THE 100K PROPERTY PLAN

THE ESSENTIAL GUIDE ON THE 'HOW TO' EARN $100,000+ A YEAR FROM PROPERTY

ANDREW CROSSLEY

First published by Busybird Publishing 2019

ISBN 978-1-925830-68-2

Ebook 978-1-925830-69-9

Cover design: Working Type Studio

Layout and typesetting: Busybird Publishing

All diagrams were created by Nicole Ellingham (Love Ginger Designs) unless otherwise specified.

busybird publishing

Busybird Publishing
2/118 Para Road
Montmorency, Victoria
Australia 3094

www.busybird.com.au

Disclaimer

The content of this book – including its strategies, ideas, concepts, explanations, definitions and opinions – do not constitute legal, financial, property, credit, compliance, or any other type of advice. All information is general in nature. Everyone's personal situation is different and expert advice must be sought in each case from a suitability-qualified individual. You will realise that this book has not taken into account your personal situation, goals, attempts at fact-finding, your risk profile, or a multitude of other factors. This book is for educational purposes and provides no warranties as to the up-to-date nature of the information contained. Risks are involved with all investments, so you must seek appropriate advice before making any decision; we disclaim all liability for any decision you may make.

I have taken every reasonable effort to ensure the accuracy of the contents in this book; however, we do not warrant or make any undertakings as to the completeness or accuracy of any information provided. Neither I nor anyone involved in this book accepts responsibility for any action that you take as a result of the motivation or education that you will hopefully receive from this book.

Contents

Acknowledgements

I would like to thank Claudia Rigoni-Brazzale (Rigale Financial Solutions).

Preface

Fear

Most people who fail in property investment do so due to fear. Fear leads to inaction, not purchasing well, not employing the right professionals to help, or not building a large enough property portfolio.

People are far too often hindered from acting by their own fear. They are their own worst enemy. 'Would be' borrowers listen to their parents and friends' opinions about where to apply for a loan, where they should purchase an investment, and where they should live. Even factors such as whether they should have a fixed rate on their mortgage or leave it variable, or the length of time to fix the rate (if they are told to fix it), or how great an offset account is may also come up in the conversation.

The best advice I can provide is to pretend to be interested in what your friends or families think. Humour them, and then ignore most, if not all, of what they say, unless your friend or family member has over six properties (approximately 0.8% of people in Australia own six properties or more), or is a successful mortgage broker. Even then, it depends on the topic of their advice (e.g. mortgage brokers cannot give advice on property unless they are suitably qualified). Likewise, if someone you know works for a bank and tries to give you advice, ignore them. They may only know their own products. I have seen so many people who used to work for a bank who become conditioned in thinking the greater world of finance mirrors the one they were surrounded with, and they struggle to comprehend the vast differences in lending policies out there.

This book will mentor you through the process of not only knowing what to do when thinking about buying an investment property, but also how to massively reduce the risk and improve the potential with every property purchase. Every successful investor has a plan. They follow it, they take action to implement it, and they have a team around them to continually advise them.

A smart investor will not just focus on capital growth; the risk of this approach is they might become a slave to the cost of debt of their portfolio, and have to keep working just to make repayments to feed the negatively geared nature of a capital growth focus portfolio. They could have sleepless nights if interest rates go up, or if one or two of their properties are vacant. An intelligent investor will not just focus on positive cash flow either, as they will likely achieve less capital growth over time and, therefore, less wealth in the future. They may have less 'growing equity' in their properties to use towards future purchases.

Too many authors and other professionals promote only one strategy, such as capital growth in blue chip suburbs, or positive cash flow in regional locations. Of course, the best solution is to buy a capital growth property with excellent cash flow, enhanced by the opportunity to manufacture more growth and cash flow within the property yourself, in blue chip suburbs near major infrastructure hubs (preferably near the Melbourne or Sydney CBDs). This is difficult to do. Rarely, if ever, can you find a positive cash flow property with great capital growth potential, near Sydney or Melbourne, within the typical budget.

The reality is that not everyone can afford to buy a capital growth property at blue chip suburb prices. The idealists out there, who promote only buying in blue chip suburbs or only buying capital growth focused properties, are just that: idealists, not realists. Their logic is perfect, in theory, but it is disconnected from the reality of the vast majority of society.

Investing with capital growth as a focus will provide a better outcome, more wealth, and a more secure retirement. This is undisputed and anyone who thinks differently is misguided. However, most investors do not earn enough to afford five to seven properties in blue chip suburbs without regard for cash flow. Most 'would be' investors do not earn 250K or more each year. They do not necessarily rate their job stability as ten out of ten, they have some fear or trepidation, and require help to invest in a practical fashion which suits them and their specific needs, not an ideological single strategy.

The obvious start is budget, loan approval, and research, then finding a location and the right property.

Having the right team around you is the most important thing you can do.

If you understand the importance of

- *not blindly trusting a real estate agent representing the seller, or a property marketing company which also represents the seller (developer) when buying a property*
- *learning to appreciate the benefit of a buyer's agent, and the invaluable reduction in risk that could be achieved by using a property advisor*
- *learning how to properly research an area to live in or to invest in*

then this book has been worth its weight in gold many times over.

Most people understand they should invest towards their future, whether by purchasing a property to live in or an investment property, just to get a foothold in the property market. Unfortunately, too many people seem to think their superannuation will provide adequate income for them in retirement, or they think there is always tomorrow and they do not need to act now. Waiting and procrastinating can be your downfall.

There is always a reason not to invest. The perceived risk of things like another global financial crisis, the property bubble bursting, removal of negative gearing, and interest rates rising scares potential investors away, yet property just keeps on rising in value over time. It is more expensive now than ten years ago, and prices ten years ago were higher than twenty years ago. This is true of every good location in Australia. Every society is full of clowns, misfits, and irrational naysayers.

If you cannot borrow or save any money, this book is not for you. This book is for people who do not spend everything they make, and who do not have an overwhelming level of debt currently. They are disciplined, motivated, and earn enough to create a balance between living in the present and living in the future. Bear in mind, some people do not know if they earn enough to be able to borrow for an investment, so please find out first, rather than making any premature assumptions.

The choice is yours. If you want to know more about reducing risk and improving potential, then read on. If you do not, or you think you know enough, then put the book down, put your head back in the sand, and I wish you luck. You may need it.

About this Book

This book, as the title suggests, discusses how having a property plan can equip you with the tools and knowledge to help build a property portfolio that can provide 100K or more passive income per year, year after year (a passive income is an income that is earned without being actively involved).

We all need money to live off in retirement. Roughly 80% or more of Australians are relegated to survive on the pension. I say 'relegated' because I believe life is to enjoy, experience, and travel. It is not, in my opinion, a mere existence spent counting pennies in retirement. Life is not about working from age eighteen to age seventy, only to then realise you miscalculated what you needed in retirement and misguidedly focused only on today and not tomorrow (metaphorically speaking). Many people in retirement lack the financial capability to do more with their life than they currently are.

Having a plan is better than haphazardly making our way through life. Taking the time to truly understand, or at least appreciate, our own situation and what our needs and wants may be now and in the future can enable you to enjoy a fuller life. Some people are arguably content going to the RSL every Friday night for a senior's meal and playing bingo every Wednesday. These simple, weekly events are what some people look forward to, and that is fine, but wouldn't it be nice to be able to help your kids, grandkids, and worthy causes – not just with your time, but also with your money?

While it is important to have a financially secure retirement, it is also about reaching a point in life, before retirement age, where you can have more choices to reduce your working hours, quit your job, or travel. It is about having hope, waking up every day, knowing you are doing everything you can to change your life for the better. Whilst daily routine is good for most of us, it can be a comfort blanket we rely on. Having several routines other than just getting up, going to work, eating dinner, putting the kids to bed, and taking the kids to their sports and activities is so important. It gives us hope that there is more out there that we can accomplish.

My goal in this book is to break down my twenty-two years of experience, qualifications, knowledge, and awards into language you can understand and implement. I have a great system and blueprint to guide you through the necessary steps, and more importantly, I have made these very easy to understand.

Financial planners write plans every day for people wanting to prepare for the future. These plans include factors such as superannuation, shares, managed funds, and insurances. A basic plan will normally not include property. While some people's financial situation is not conducive to property, good financial planners will include an allocation of funds towards property as an asset class, even though they do not receive a commission on property (hence what makes them good financial planners; they look after the client, not their back pocket).

If a financial planner includes property in a financial plan, it would not include specific property. ASIC (Australian Securities and Investments Commission) do not consider property as an investment security and it does not fall under a financial services license, meaning it falls outside the area which someone with a financial services license can advise on. Therefore, you need to use a property advisor to provide you with a property investment plan, not a financial planner.

I am not going to touch on any asset class except property. Property allows you to also have a well-diversified portfolio.

This book is not for the wealthy or already successful people in property either. The very wealthy amongst us most likely already have a diversified portfolio, across several asset classes. Their investments are not in one sector, one property class, one property type, or one location or strategy. Typically, their portfolio may have 65–70% in residential property, and 30–35% in commercial or industrial property. Their residential portfolio may contain their principal place of residence, a holiday house or short-term holiday let, and potentially a couple of well-positioned properties in the capital cities down the Eastern seaboard of Australia. Remember, these investors are not successful because they were born with more knowledge; it is because they have advisors and they have a plan.

'Mum and dad investors' who want to better their future with less risk of negatively impacting on their present will benefit more from this book. Everything you will read is not only aimed at a positive outcome in the future, but it is also aimed at providing an outcome today, tomorrow, and during the time the portfolio is growing with less risk of negatively impacting on lifestyle. There must be a balance between enjoying life now and enjoying life in the future, before and after retirement.

I hope to impress upon you what a plan may look like, and the importance of having one. "Without a plan, you plan to fail." Many of you would be aware of this saying, but it is often not taken seriously enough. You must have goals. You need to understand what is possible, and then know how best to make choices in order to maximise the outcome for yourself.

Most people do not have the means to achieve what the very wealthy have. However, if they live responsibly with enough equity in their home or money put aside (if they do not own a property), have an average salary or higher, and can manage their debt, then they can get ahead in life. Once someone starts to build assets, they can begin to leverage off those assets and it gets easier to get ahead, provided that they do things properly. This book covers what 'properly' entails. It also covers why it is important to use a buyer's agent and never rely on a real estate agent or property marketing company. I feel sorry for someone if they purchased 'direct' from a property marketing company at a seminar or any other situation without an intermediary analysing the property versus other choices. Seek advice from a qualified professional, with the goal of achieving some of what the wealthy have.

Research is the most important thing that you must do before investing in anything, especially property. Key points when researching for a principal place of residence and/or an investment property are covered in this book, as I believe looking for a principal place of residence can be just as important, if not more, than searching for an investment (albeit, with a strikingly different set of criteria). The extent of many people's research is flicking through all the pretty pictures on realestate.com or domain.com. This is part of the research process, but it is one of the last parts, not the first or only part. There are several steps you must follow before getting to the point of looking at what is for sale. These many steps will be explained.

Finance is crucial, and to get it right can be difficult. Just like building a portfolio, you must have a plan, consisting of several strategies. My second book, *Property Finance Made Simple*, is a must-read; this book contains new and updated information you need to know on how to improve your borrowing capacity, what you need to consider when applying for a loan, and finance strategies to enable you to potentially purchase more property.

Half of the people who own an investment property in Australia sell their investment property in the first five years, which means half of all investors are doing themselves an injustice. Their definition of 'commitment to self' is very grey. Investing in property is not for everyone; it is for people who are sincere and committed to making a difference for themselves and for their family in the future.

It is not just about the future, though. A friend of mine ended up owning six properties by the age of forty-five. They then sold a property each time one of their four children entered high school. The school fees were roughly 30K p.a. The equity in four of the six properties combined covered the six years of annual fees for the four children. It also allowed them to go on a round-the-world trip once the kids graduated. They still had two properties, and are rebuilding their portfolio.

Another friend rented for many years and purchased three properties. They had one child and continued to rent. When their second child was on the way, they decided it was time to buy their dream house. Selling their three investment properties provided them the equity for a sizable deposit on the house they wanted. This provided two solutions: one was the house itself, and the other was a low enough loan against the house to give them instant equity in the house, which meant they were able to leverage off it and start investing again.

Investing is not just for retirement; it is to have choices in ten, fifteen, or twenty years. It is also for hope. It fuels dreams and makes them more likely. Without hope, a dream, or a goal, what is the point?

My recent book, *The Australian Property Investment Handbook 2018/19*, provided an invaluable blueprint on what you should consider doing every time you purchase an investment property. I have included a copy of the blueprint in this book, but I recommend you refer to *The Australian Property Investment Handbook 2018/19* for a descriptive understanding and explanation of the blueprint. This book builds on that framework and provides you with an invaluable source of knowledge, no matter what your situation; whether it be that you do not have an investment property, or you already have several properties and simply do not know what to do next.

There are three words I live by and I believe you should too: 'Commitment to self'

If someone does not have a goal, nor consider each move after the next like in a game of chess or snooker, they could become snookered or 'check mated' in life. They could look back with hindsight and see that they failed to commit to themselves and their family.

Some people, after reading this book, will get excited for a day or a week, similar to what happens after attending a seminar or reading a self-help book, only to become distracted and entrenched back into the routine of life once again. Some people are not, and will not be, in a position to achieve their goals, maybe due to the inability to borrow money, too much debt, too many kids, not having enough money saved, not having enough interest in property, or not being goal-orientated or focused on the future. But, if I can make a difference with this book, and either save some people from themselves, or help others take the next step towards buying a property by not only having followed the information in this book, but also having sought advice from a qualified professional, then that is fantastic. I will have made a difference and that is all I can ask for.

The differences I hope to make are the following:

- *Provide information and examples on a tailored plan, aimed at getting back on track to achieving set goals*
- *Provide information to protect you from sales agents*
- *Save you time*
- *Save you money*
- *Help you to overcome fear and avoid frustration*
- *Help you focus on tomorrow without negatively affecting today.*

At some point in the future you will stop work and still need income. The level of income you receive then depends entirely on you, your needs, your commitment to yourself and your family, and your ability to act on the commitment you have made. Most of us want more and want what is best, but may not know how to go about it, so this book will help you. Your level of success does not determine your commitment to your family, but your level of effort towards considering the future does.

The question you need to be honest with yourself about is: do you have the knowledge or experience to do everything yourself?

To build, or start to build, a property portfolio in as much of a stress-free manner as possible, I recommend you always refer back to this book, and have a team of professionals around you. This excludes a real estate agent and/or property marketing company. If you wish to have further assistance, because you do not have time to do it yourself, or you are concerned about doing it yourself, I recommend you contact me at www.Australianpropertyadvisorygroup.com.au (APAG) to work with you each step of the way.

This book contains property investment strategies and a tailored plan for a family scenario that is fairly common in Australia. It also contains a blueprint on property advice, buyer advocacy services, and knowledge on must-know research.

Many people in Australia under the age of forty struggle to invest in more than one or two properties, if that. Many others struggle with investing after the age of fifty-five if they have not already. Maybe they think it is too late, or there is an ingrained fear of risk.

There is a six-step process in developing a plan. This is what my blueprint is all about. Refer to Chapter One for Step One. Chapter Two, which is about Step Two, is the most important part of the book. This chapter details what a plan would look like in an example scenario designed to represent the majority of people in Australia.

Chapter 3 will go through Step 4 in detail, while Chapter 4 will go through Step 5 in detail.-Chapter 5 brings all of these steps together. My newly published book *Commercial Property and Residential Development Made Simple* is written about Steps 3 and 6; specifically, about the buying process. It is a how-to guide to having more success in supercharging your capital growth and cash flow.

The revised edition of my previous book, *Property Investing Made Simple,* covers all of your other potential questions about property managers, quantity surveyors, property inspection, and much more. Read *Property Finance Made Simple* to better understand what you can do to improve your situation in a lender's eyes. Having a pre-approval makes you more able to jump at an opportunity.

Other Books by Andrew Crossley

Property Investing Made Simple
www.propertyinvestingmadesimple.com.au

Property Finance Made Simple
www.propertyfinancemadesimple.net.au

The Australian Property Investment Handbook 2018/19
www.thehandbook.com.au

Commercial Property and Residential Development Made Simple
www.the100kpropertyplan.com.au

Children's books:

Billy and Harry love to play

Billy and Harry go to the zoo

Billy and Harry go to the beach

Billy and Harry go camping

Billy and Harry go on a winter holiday

Billy and Harry go to the playground
www.billyandharry.com.au

About the Author

Andrew Crossley lives in Melbourne, and is the #1 bestselling and award-winning author of three books: *Property Investing Made Simple, Property Finance Made Simple,* and *The Australian Property Investment Handbook 2018/19. The 100K Property Plan* is his fourth book in the *Made Simple* series. He has also written a children's book, entitled *Billy and Harry love to play.*

Andrew has worked in the Finance and Property industry for over twenty-two years, thirteen of those years in Australia. This included working for the largest non-bank and the largest mortgage manager in Australia during that time. He has also worked overseas in private wealth management on several continents.

Andrew is the founder of Australian Property Advisory Group (APAG), a buyer advocacy and property advisory business based in Melbourne, servicing all of Australia. APAG's buyer advocacy services specialise in working with investors, rather than people looking for a place to live, to reduce risk and improve potential with every investment property purchase. This is achieved through thorough research, leading to the shortlisting of 'where to buy,' sourcing of investment grade properties (the 'what to buy' to rent easily and remain in demand), and negotiation. APAG believes negotiating on a client's behalf will improve the chances of obtaining the property at a better price than what a client could do themselves, due to extensive negotiation and buying experience, often leading to a greater chance of saving the equivalent of the buyer's advocacy fee.

APAG offers tailor-made solutions and customised property investment plans to help investors, based on their current situation and their future goals, grow a portfolio which is well-balanced and affordable to maintain. Every person has a goal to retire comfortably and to have options available to them prior to retirement, whether to do volunteer work, travel more, or cut back on working hours. A tailored plan can provide a more achievable outcome than just buying an investment property and hoping for the best, or buying several properties without them being aligned to your circumstances and each other.

APAG was a finalist in the 2016 Australian Small Business Awards, highly recommended in the 2015 Investors Choice Awards in the categories of Property Investment Advisor and Buyer's Agent, and was national runner-up in the prestigious 2015 Readers' Choice Awards.

Property Industry Awards:

- *Finalist (Highly Recommended): Best Buyer's Agent in Australia, Readers' Choice Awards, 2016*
- *Runner Up: Best Buyer's Agent in Australia, Readers' Choice Awards, 2015*
- *Highly Recommended: Buyer's Agent, Investors Choice Awards, 2015*
- *Highly Recommended: Property Investment Advisor, Investors Choice Awards, 2015*

Finance Industry Awards:

- *NATIONAL WINNER: Australian Mortgage Awards (AMA), 2018*

- *NATIONAL WINNER: Mortgage and Finance Association of Australia (MFAA), 2017*
- *STATE WINNER: Mortgage and Finance Association of Australia (MFAA), 2017*
- *Finalist: Better Business Awards, 2017*
- *Finalist: Mortgage and Finance Association of Australia (MFAA), 2016*
- *Finalist: Mortgage and Finance Association of Australia (MFAA), 2015*
- *Finalist: Mortgage and Finance Association of Australia (MFAA), 2014*
- *Finalist: Australian Mortgage Awards, 2016*
- *Finalist: Australian Mortgage Awards, 2015*

Book Awards and Milestones:

Property Investing Made Simple

- *#1 Bestseller*
- *Best book: 'Real Estate' category, International Book Awards, 2015*
- *Best book: 'Real Estate' category, Book Excellence Awards, 2016*

Property Finance Made Simple

- *#1 Bestseller and #67 in all books on Amazon Kindle Australia*

The Australian Property Investment Handbook 2018/19

- *#1 Bestseller and #68 in all books on Amazon Kindle Australia*

Qualifications:

- Accredited Property Investment Advisor, Property Investment Professionals of Australia (PIPA)
- Qualified Property Investment Advisor (QPIA)
- Fully licensed Real Estate Agent (NSW and VIC)
- Advanced Diploma in Financial Services (Financial Planning)
- Diploma in Finance (Mortgage Broking Management)
- Masters in Business Administration
- Masters in Commerce
- Masters in Commercial Law

Andrew has also written for dozens of industry and non-industry publications, and has appeared on TV and radio. He is an educator, mentor, consultant, and public speaker.

Having grown a personal portfolio of over twelve properties, consisting of houses, townhouses, dual occupancies, and units across several states, Andrew was recognised in the *Your Investment Property Magazine* Property Investor of the Year Awards, 2012.

Personal Message:

I am sure you will enjoy reading my book as much as I have enjoyed writing it and sharing my knowledge and insights with you. Whether buying your first investment property or your next, it should be a worthwhile experience. To help ensure that it is an enjoyable experience, you need to arm yourself with the right information, then implement that information and use professionals in their fields to help you.

Blueprint

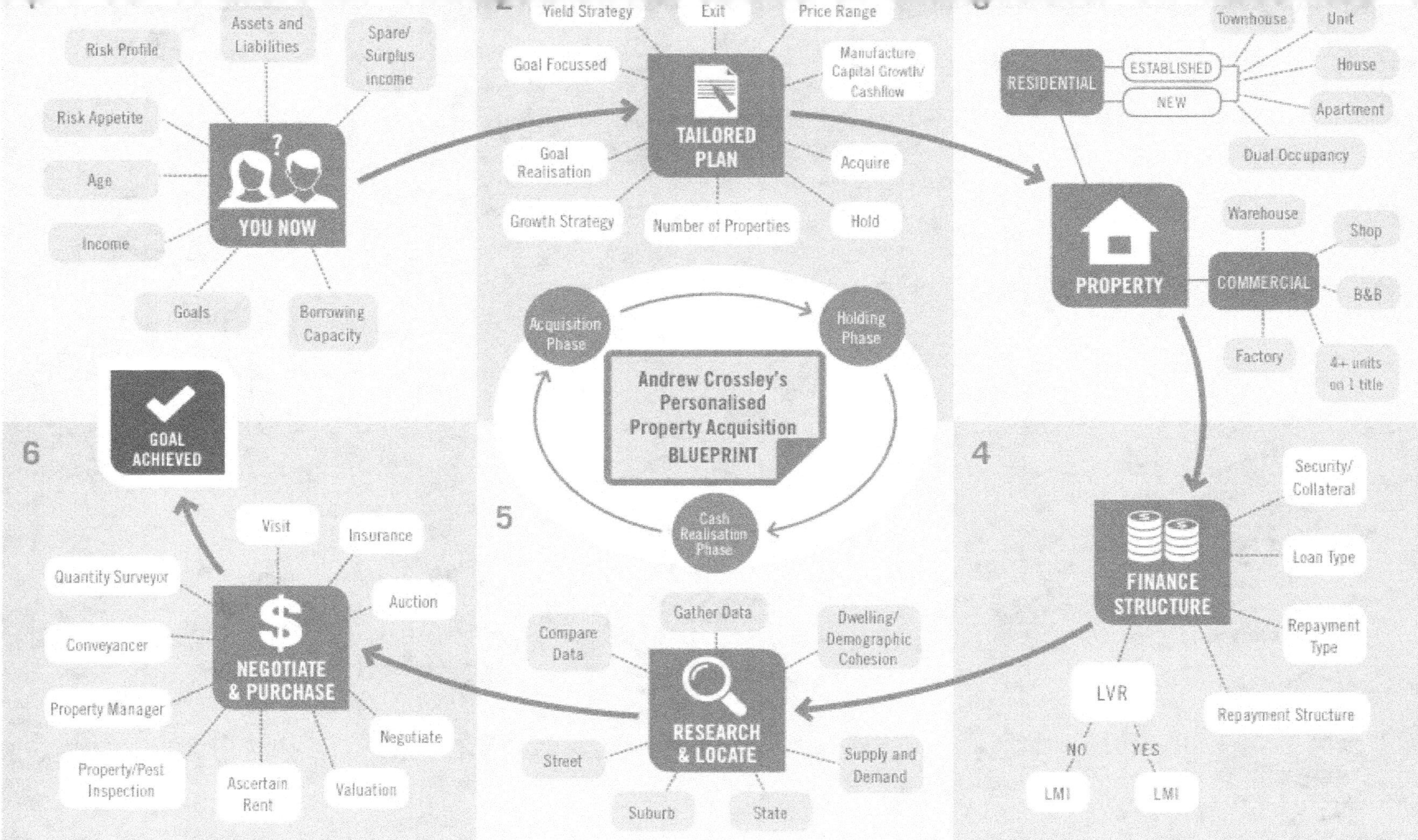

YOU NOW
Risk Profile
Assets and Liabilities
Spare/ Surplus income
Risk Appetite
Age
Income
Goals
Borrowing Capacity
TAILORED PLAN
Yield Strategy
Exit
Price Range
Goal Focussed
Manufacture Capital Growth/ Cashflow
Goal Realisation
Acquire
Growth Strategy
Number of Properties
Hold
PROPERTY
RESIDENTIAL
ESTABLISHED
NEW
Townhouse
Unit
House
Apartment
Dual Occupancy
COMMERCIAL
Warehouse
Shop
B&B
Factory
4+ units on 1 title
4
FINANCE STRUCTURE
Security/ Collateral
Loan Type
Repayment Type
Repayment Structure
LVR
NO
YES
LMI
LMI
5
Andrew Crossley's Personalised Property Acquisition BLUEPRINT
Acquisition Phase
Holding Phase
Cash Realisation Phase
RESEARCH & LOCATE
Gather Data
Compare Data
Dwelling/ Demographic Cohesion
Street
Supply and Demand
Suburb
State
6
GOAL ACHIEVED
NEGOTIATE & PURCHASE
Visit
Insurance
Quantity Surveyor
Auction
Conveyancer
Property Manager
Negotiate
Property/Pest Inspection
Ascertain Rent
Valuation

CHAPTER 1

You, Your Current Situation, Your Capacity, and Your Goals

This chapter is all about understanding your current situation, in order to determine the chances you have of building a portfolio.

Goals

With anything you do of importance in life, it is far better to understand what you need to do before you try and achieve it. Without hope and having goals, we merely exist; there is nothing to strive for or look forward to. Having a goal gives direction and purpose, be it a small or big goal, short-term or long-term.

In order to understand what you need to do, and what goals may be realistic, more challenging, or simply unattainable, you need to understand your current situation. If you do not know where you are, you will have no idea where you need to go. It is crucial to understand the following factors, as these also contribute significantly to your ability to borrow money:

- *Assets*
- *Available equity in your home or other properties*
- *Health*
- *Stability in employment*

- *Borrowing capacity (to be obtained by a mortgage broker or bank)*
- *Income*
- *Liabilities*
- *Number of kids you have and/or may want to have*
- *Basic living expenses (e.g. rates, utilities, repairs, food, transport, fuel, parking, takeaway, clothing and personal care, cosmetics, rental costs/board, body corporate costs)*
- *Additional living expenses (e.g. investment utilities, insurance for home/contents/health/landlord/life/Total and Permanent Disablement/trauma, phone bills, internet bills, subscriptions, dental and medical bills, education fees/books/uniforms/activities, childcare, child support/ maintenance, recreation, entertainment, memberships, restaurants, holidays)*
- *Risk tolerance (this pertains to your risk appetite)*
- *Risk profile as determined by a bank or advisor (e.g. if you have too many credit cards, are living beyond your means, are unable to manage a budget, or are unable to save or put aside any money to invest, then you would more likely be considered an undesirable risk or a high-risk profile)*
- *Surplus income (what you have spare every week and month that can be allocated to owning an investment property/ies)*
- *Desired/Realistic age of retirement*

All of these things have a bearing on what can be done next, what a plan moving forward will look like, and how likely it may be to achieve the desired outcome modelled in the plan. It is important to recognise that having a plan does not guarantee an outcome, but I believe it will have a great likelihood of producing a better outcome than not having a plan.

In terms of property investment, the main goal should be a monetary one, *not* "I want ten properties in ten years." It is foolish to want ten properties; even though ten sounds good, it lacks a practical outcome. Your reason for your monetary goal can include anything, such as leaving a legacy, going on a dream holiday, upgrading your dream home using any capital gain achieved, affording private school fees, or comfortable retirement. In retirement, life comes down to survival and you need money for that.

Monetary goals can be, very simply, one of two things: capital growth or cash flow. Capital growth can be cashed in, and, after capital gains tax, it can be spent on school fees or any other goal requiring lump sums. Cash flow is also useful pre-retirement and post-retirement.

Pre-retirement, extra income allows us to do more, enjoy life, and reduce stress levels related to costs and living. Spending income, rather than capital gains, helps us maintain and afford to borrow more money for investment in property.

A useful and considered outcome comes from determining your income requirement in retirement. Retirement age can be open-ended. The younger someone starts investing, the more time those assets have to grow in value, and the more potential income can be derived from those assets later in life. Many people tend to assume that if they work hard and save money then one day they will end up wealthy. This is wishful thinking, as over 80% of people will end up on the pension. With this mindset, most people end up with a modest and ultimately less useful amount of money to live off in retirement. They are unlikely to be wealthy unless they have their own business and sell it for a couple million dollars.

An income figure could be anywhere between $40,000 to $200,000 or more p.a.; what matters is that the figure is right for you and will meet your needs. No one knows for sure, twenty years ahead of time, what their income will be, of course. Once you have a goal, you will need to work backwards from that figure. Knowing what you want and need in your retirement provides clarity and direction for the plan. Plans can evolve and be flexible, if well designed, but it is important to start with a solid foundation. Know your current situation and any threats or weaknesses to its stability. It is easier to then establish a plan of action allowing for, as best as possible, any threats or weaknesses to your current position. Usually between the ages of 45 and 65 is the best earning period in a person's life. It is easier to leverage off your assets – in particular, property – whilst you are less likely to overstretch yourself.

Age

This will impact on your ability to obtain a loan, especially if you are over fifty-five years of age. Anyone Over 55 usually requires an exit strategy when applying for a loan. The main impact, from a property perspective, is that your age will directly impact how much time you have left to work and for the investment properties in the plan to grow in value towards achieving the passive income goal. It will also impact on the viable length of the plan moving forward and the likelihood of the passive income goal being realised. Potentially, some harsh realities will be faced for some people who may have left it too late. The level of risk appropriate for someone's situation is also influenced by age. The older someone is, the less risk they may consider taking, depending on their attitude, the advice they receive, and the appropriateness of that advice and their circumstances.

Exit strategies have a direct correlation with the age of a borrower when it comes to obtaining finance. The borrower needs to show an ability to repay the loan at the time it is taken out, or, if their exit strategy is worded satisfactorily in the loan submission notes, when they cease work and retire. Submission notes are provided by a good mortgage broker to a lender on behalf of the borrower. Good luck if you do not use a broker – you will need all the luck you can get!

The type of work/industry also has a bearing on whether someone is considered able to work until 67–70 years of age. For example, if the borrower is employed in a labour-intensive role, they are unlikely to work as long as someone in an office or administrative role. In an office, there is less wear and tear on the body; therefore, a person in an office or administrative role would potentially work for a few more years. However, if an office worker eats too many donuts, for example, and becomes obese, this could also impact on their ability to keep working to age 70.

Lenders may offer the option of a shorter loan term to coincide with the time when the borrower turns seventy, particularly if the borrower is over sixty years old (it is difficult for a lender to provide the borrower a 30-year loan term if it is likely that the borrower will be dead prior to the end of the loan term). A shorter loan term means the amortised repayments (costs of monthly mortgage repayments which are condensed into a shorter time frame) can therefore be much higher. This can easily lead to the person appearing unable to demonstrate the ability to afford the loan.

A more popular or easily acceptable strategy, depending on whether you talk to the lender or the borrower, is demonstrating enough equity in investment properties or value in shares equivalent to the loan amount being sought, therefore proving the ability to pay off the loan. This needs to be demonstrated at the time the loan is being assessed. Banks do not like people masquerading as economists and property experts by saying that their property will grow to a certain value in the future; they do not like using speculation in this way. Telling the lender additional repayments will be made to pay down the debt are not normally acceptable either, as this is hearsay and speculation. I have purposely left superannuation out of the definition of assets, because lenders are starting to not accept the amount someone has in their super fund as relevant to an exit strategy. Lenders believe that superannuation should be used as a source of income in retirement, not as a cash cow to waste paying off debt, leaving nothing for the person to derive an income from in retirement.

The strategy of downsizing to a smaller property is often considered a bit of a throwaway line that applicants use far too often to try and demonstrate an exit strategy. Downsizing can work with some lenders if there is enough equity in the property, at the time of the loan being applied for, to afford a respectable property in a similar area. If the borrower suggests they will downsize from an area like Toorak, Victoria to Moe, Victoria (quite a difference in property price and demographic), a lender may not consider this acceptable. The lender could regard this as too much of a downgrade from the lifestyle the borrower is accustomed to. However, if they have relatives in Moe, for example, then this can aid in supporting the reality of their claim. It is considered a throwaway line when someone has a 400K property with a 320K debt on the property, and they say they will downsize. Caravans, tents, nursing homes, or moving in with kids are at the least unacceptable, and at the most, stupid and unrealistic (particularly in the case of the tent – glamping style – which I have seen used on a couple of occasions).

Borrowers may also nominate, if they are self-employed, that they are planning to sell their business. Lenders do not want to be complicit or implicated in a situation where someone is required to put in motion this downsizing or selling of business proposition. It could be construed in a court of law that they are being forced by the bank to sell their house or business. People change their minds as they get older, and may not want to sell their business or move out of the family home anymore. They could easily twist the situation around, and say how unfair it is that the 'big bad lender' is doing this to them. They could suddenly end up as a hard done by story on a so-called 'current affairs' program, where someone is saying they are being sold-up by a bank.

In the case of selling a business, a bank/lender is not a business valuer. Any stated value of a business has too much risk of being unsubstantiated or inflated, and there is certainly no guarantee of the worth of the business ten years down the track. Besides, lenders will not want to be involved in a person removing themselves from their source of income.

There are cases where a person has said they would downsize, then they get sick and cannot work anymore. The lender is then called to task for wanting repayments to continue or the exit strategy to be fulfilled. It is best for lenders to avoid these situations, especially now that we have lenders exercising their own interpretation of legislation on responsible lending practices.

If a thirty-year-old and their parent go on the loan, and the parent is over fifty-five years of age, the parent will, most of the time, need to demonstrate an exit strategy equivalent to be able to pay out the entire debt, independent of the co-borrower if the co-borrower is anyone but their partner (de facto or married). If two people are over fifty-five years of age and not in a relationship, then they each must have the ability to pay out the entire loan independent of the other.

Assets

If you do not have any assets, your credit score may end up being quite low. Most lenders use a credit score system (refer to my book *Property Finance Made Simple*, where credit scoring is explained). It is worth noting that a few lenders do not credit score and can lend up to 95% loan to value ratio without credit scoring. The assets you do have, from a property investment plan perspective, will contribute to the plan in a crucial manner. The amount of accessible equity in the assets influences the plan from its inception all the way through to the modelled outcome. The more available equity in a property, the more money there is to use as a deposit for the next property investment purchase.

Let's use an example: borrowing 80% of the purchase price of an investment property. No lender will loan 100%, so you will have to put in some money. It is normally 10–20% for a standard property, and 30% if you are an expat or buying an inner city apartment or serviced apartment.

Purchase for 600K

Borrow amount 80% = 480K

Input amount is 20% = 120K + costs of 5% (which is mainly stamp duty) = 30K (if it is an established property. Stamp duty on a Not Yet Built property could be considerably less).

Total money required = 150K

The more properties that need to be purchased in the plan, the more cash, shares, or available equity in existing properties there needs to be (or family members prepared to gift the money, but let's not count on that).

In this example, the money required to purchase an investment property with a sale price of 600K, borrowing 80%, will be 150K. Borrowing 90% against the investment property will preserve any available equity in other properties and the total amount required would drop from 150K to 90K.

Borrowing Capacity

There are three elements that influence the level of affordability for a borrower: price, the income of the borrower, and interest rates. Lenders, on the back of the pressure applied by APRA (Australian Prudential Regulation Authority), have implemented a number of changes that have indirectly led to people's ability to borrow money becoming more difficult. Lenders, broadly speaking, usually apply a variable interest rate to a loan based on the purpose of the loan. If the purpose is investment, the rate is often higher than if the purpose was to purchase a property to live in.

Interest-only loans are then priced even higher than principal and interest repayments on investment and owner-occupied purpose loans. Some lenders price on the security the debt is against. So, for example, you could have business debt, investment debt, and owner-occupier purpose debt against the principal place of residence, and the rate could be as low as the mid to high 3% range. The difference between the loan purpose, the repayment type, and lender you choose will make a difference of up to or more than 1% on the interest rate, so speak to a good mortgage broker.

Income

Your income will determine how much you can borrow. It also forms part of what you can afford to spend and save, and it impacts on what you can contribute to an investment property. The level of income will also have a bearing on the property investment plan. For example, all other things being equal, the higher the income, the more someone can borrow, the more debt can be afforded. Someone on a very high income may benefit more from a capital growth focused property rather than a positive cash flow focused property.

The reality is that not all other things are equal, so everything about the person must be assessed to determine the best strategy. The borrower may spend most of what they make. They may already have several properties, other expenses, or be on principal and interest payments on several debts. So, in some cases, higher income earners may still be in need of a property producing a higher yield rather than more capital growth. Yield versus rental, in dollar terms, will be covered later on.

Your Living Expenses

This impacts on the level of debt you can afford, your borrowing capacity, and the amount you can save. Lenders are placing an ever-increasing significance on this. In fact, besides your income, this is one of the greatest variables, and every lender treats your living expenses differently. Lenders have been increasing the applied living expenses in their borrowing capacity calculators, and have become more particular and granular in their analysis of living expenses.

Liabilities

The amount of debt you have will also impact on what can be borrowed. The more credit cards a household has, the worse off their borrowing capacity is. HECS debt (now known as HELP, Higher Education Loan Program), child maintenance, personal loans, whether any mortgages are on principal and interest payments versus interest-only payments, and the number of children in the household will all come to bear on the borrowing capacity calculator of a bank. The severity of how negatively impacted a borrower will be by having the above debts is covered in my book *Property Finance Made Simple.*

Historically, lenders' borrowing capacity calculators would assess the repayments a person was making. Now, however, the majority of lenders do not care if a person is making interest-only or principal and interest repayments on their existing debts; the calculator will convert interest-only repayments as if they were principal and interest, and then add a buffer of roughly 2–4%, equating to a typical qualifying rate of around 7.25%, sometimes up to 8%.

Your Surplus/Spare Income

This will not only contribute to what the plan needs to look like, and what is possibly achievable. It is also a key factor of whether a plan is viable. If a property investor – or a 'would be' property investor – cannot put aside any money per week, they should think carefully about whether buying a property is right for them.

Some real estate agents and many property marketing companies will try to sell you on the concept of positive cash flow properties; please bear in mind that there is no guarantee the property will not be vacant. There is never a guarantee the tenant will pay on time, or continue to pay. God forbid if you are misled into buying in a one-horse town (also known as a one-industry town), or a town with a population of a few hundred or thousand. You are almost guaranteed of losing in the long run.

Every property has unexpected expenses over time, and investors must be prepared for a property costing more than the income they are receiving. Interest rates have been and may continue going up. Loans will not be interest-only forever; when they convert to principal and interest, the cost of the loan may go up 40% or more.

If you need to purchase a capital growth focused property, then often by default it will be negatively geared, and you would need to afford the higher out of pocket cost. The Government has now intentionally made it more difficult for you to afford an established property, given you can no longer claim any depreciation on any fixtures and fittings that came with the property.

Surplus income will have an important bearing on the:

- *Type of properties modelled in the plan*
- *Number of properties*
- *Relevant strategy with each property*
- *Interest-only or principal and interest repayments*
- *Price of the property*
- *New versus established property*
- *When each property is purchased*
- *The holding period for each property*

Of course, everything in this section has an impact on these choices, but, ultimately, it can come down to something so simple as the amount you can put aside each week.

Risk Appetite and Risk Profile

Risk is the chance that an investment will not provide the returns hoped for. You could lose some or all of your money, or not make any money. All investments involve risk, but some are riskier than others.

Higher risk investments are often more likely to produce higher returns over time than more conservative investments. Over short periods of time, investments of any kind can fall in value. Property is a long-term, not short-term, investment, unless you plan to develop or renovate the property. With a buy and hold strategy, it is certainly a long-term strategy.

A risk profile and appetite are important to understand for both you and your advisor. As mentioned earlier, a good advisor will probably not want to work with a client who has a high-risk profile. People who mismanage their debts, miss their debt repayments, or are over their head in debt are not ideal candidates for taking on more.

The risk appetite of a buyer can often get in the way of that person investing. There are a number of factors that can explain why many people have not invested in property yet, have only purchased one or two properties, or have failed to build a property portfolio. The most common factors are fear and analysis paralysis. With these two factors, I recommend reading the final chapter in my book *Property Investing Made Simple.*

Other factors include not knowing who to trust, being time poor, lack of knowledge, and financial constraints. The buyer's risk appetite is often something only the buyer can deal with if their reason for not investing is fear. Many other reasons for not investing can be dealt with, or better understood and hopefully overcome with the help of a good advisor.

Once a buyer has decided they are willing to invest in property, their risk profile will determine what their property plan looks like, and what this personalised strategy could then provide can be calculated. Each type of strategy, location, and property has its own risks and benefits. A property buyer or potential buyer's risk appetite can be used to assist with trying to choose a strategy and property more suited to their individual needs.

There are some questions that are general in nature, but can help guide an investor and their advisor to gain a better understanding of the buyer's risk profile and appetite. Questions can often vary across different advisory industries.

One such question to ask is ascertaining if the investor would retain their investment in the property for more than two years if it was performing badly. Given the long-term nature of property, it could arguably be appropriate to hold for much longer than two years if the suburb and driving factors of growth support it. But if some mining town fails in QLD or WA, for example, it may be foolish to sit and wait for things to turn around. Assess each situation on its own merit, but, generally, an investment needs to be held for more than two years (provided that, from the outset, it was acquired on the back of thorough research).

A willingness to risk a percentage of income to seek a good return on a property investment would support the view that the buyer understands that there is risk, and they accept it is worth risking some money. This is contrary to the alternative: if the potential buyer did not want to risk any money, they will probably remain a *potential* buyer, and never progress to be a buyer.

When deciding whether to invest in property, an analysis is undertaken on the possible losses compared to the possible capital growth. If the level of focus is more on the losses than the potential capital growth, the buyer would probably have a lower risk appetite. It is good to weigh potential losses against potential gains, but when undertaking a decision in a well-thought-out manner, worrying about losses should hopefully be minimalised. Do not forget these questions are at the start of the research process; they are not used when comparing one property against another.

The level of conservatism of an investor can be gauged if the investor would like to rely on a 'guaranteed' capital growth, rather than accepting a level of uncertainty. It is important to understand that no amount of capital growth can ever be guaranteed. A buyer may be better off putting their head in the bottomless sandpit of denial, and remaining embedded in their own little world if they are waiting around for a guarantee. Dealing with levels of uncertainty requires knowledge and experience, both of which a buyer can leverage off with a suitably qualified professional advisor and thorough research. There is always uncertainty, as there is no crystal ball or guarantee. One cannot eliminate risk or control the future, but risk can be reduced, and the level of potential capital gain can be improved.

People like to make comparisons to others, either to reinforce feeling good about themselves, or to stimulate themselves in trying harder. So, it is reasonable to think about whether you take more risk than the average person. It is difficult to have clear perspective here, but consider this: do you consider yourself average? Do you want to be average? The good thing for those of us that want more in life is that there are enough people wanting to just be average, which means there is opportunity for others to strive to be better than average. Most people only ever buy one investment property in their life. If this is all you would like to do, then having a plan is a waste of time. A plan is for someone who can and wants to achieve more for their future.

If a person would rather deposit their money in a bank than invest, they are a low risk appetite person. Money in a bank will not build wealth, nor provide any leverage.

Financial uncertainty is scary for many people. If a property buyer recognises that there is uncertainty with property – and any other investment, for that matter – but appreciates it is possible to minimise this uncertainty, then this is a positive outcome.

The level of acceptance of short-term losses in order to pursue long-term investment growth is an important indicator of an investor's appetite to invest. If the investor does not want to accept that property can go up and down in the short term, and they do not have the patience to wait for growth to be realised on a property with a buy and hold strategy, then they should consider that property investing may not be for them.

It is worth noting that property growth runs in cycles; it can level off, drop in value, or rise in value in the short term, but over ten to fifteen years, property values in decent areas can often double in value. Property has typically doubled in every seven- to ten-year cycle. It is arguably more prudent to not rely on this achievement repeating itself, but rather to allow potentially fifteen years for properties to double in value.

Some people may be more aggressive or assertive in how they wish to move forward, sometimes from desperation or out of sheer necessity. However, a plan moving forward needs to be justified and responsible, managing your expectations and avoiding becoming a slave to your debt. Sometimes a risk appetite does not correlate to a risk profile. For example, a couple who has more than four credit cards may be a higher-risk profile, but may have a very low risk appetite. Some 'would be' property investors have a higher risk appetite than what they should have for their circumstances. This can end up putting them in a precarious situation, exposing them to an untenable future cost of debt.

Needs will vary depending on experience, knowledge, and risk profile. Less experienced buyers generally want someone to manage the process for them, and help them find a property. Intelligent, experienced property investors already appreciate the importance of a personal, suitably qualified property advisor.

If someone wants a positive cash flow property, this tends to suit lower risk appetites, preferring not to take the risk of being too negatively geared or waiting ten to fifteen years for an increase in value. Perhaps their health or job security is unpredictable, such that it is preferable not to be out of pocket too much. Capital growth strategies may require a slightly higher risk appetite, as the buyer will probably have to wait for the growth, whilst earning less from the property.

Social Demographics

Society can be broken down into several broad holistic groups. This is not an exact science and do not feel pigeonholed when you read the next section. You may fall into one of these groups, or you may be an exception to the rule. Generally, these categories attempt to capture everyone over the age of eighteen.

Young: Younger generations of people who just turned eighteen or are slightly older. They are starting out in life and not sure where they are headed, concentrating on university and accumulating a HELP debt, travelling, or they simply have other priorities rather than investing.

Battlers: There are those that unfortunately will never or are unlikely to ever be in a financial position to own their own home, let alone invest in a second property.

Interested/Aspiring: These people have not yet invested, for several understandable reasons, such as short-term or previous financial constraints, being time poor, not knowing who to trust, lack of knowledge, analysis paralysis, and – the biggest culprit of them all – fear.

Talkers: The talkers sit there with their other talker friends, chatting about how much they know about property. They assure each other that prices will go down, how there is a property bubble, why it is better to wait and see, that it is not a good time to buy now, or they just want to see what the market does. They may hold court in their fanciful mansion in the middle of a suburb where the median house price is under 500K. They feel like a king in their own little world. They surround themselves with fellow talkers so they do not feel lonely in their inaction. They are destined to become the next generation of the 'coulda, woulda, shoulda' crowd. This 'coulda, woulda, shoulda' crowd used to be the talkers; now they are just the jaded group that regret what they did not do when they had the chance.

Starters: They may have one property or two. They may or may not have had previous financial constraints. They may not know how to move forward or keep progressing with their property portfolio. They may be too time poor to continue. They have started investing, but need help and do not know where to go or who to trust. Their lack of knowledge sets in, as they have realised they do not know what or where to buy next. Maybe they purchased an investment property near to where they live because it provided them comfort and familiarity, and they have been lucky to live in an area that has done very well. They may also be scared to expose themselves to more debt because they are already negatively geared to the limit of their comfort level. Perhaps their property has not performed, or they lost money because they listened to those capricious, slick talking property marketing companies and purchased in areas like Gladstone, QLD or Moranbah, QLD.

Note: There is someone in the property industry I know of who sells properties in areas that developers are going hell for leather in. Then, just like the movie *Independence Day*, he, like the aliens, moves to another planet (or in this case, another area) to sell property and destroy that area, creating another situation of oversupply. All the while, saying how good it is, he takes advantage of the next keen mum and dad investor who can only spend 400–450K on an investment property.

Doers: There are two kinds of doers. They have two or more properties and are unafraid. The first kind still seek guidance (which is great). They have done well, they want to build on what they have, and often seek advice from a suitably qualified professional. Others continue along, happy as can be, full of hope with their dreams still alive. Some, though, have overly negatively geared themselves. They will learn they have done so in a normal interest rate market, or when their interest rates change to principal and interest repayments from interest-only.

Existers: This group was touched on in the 'About this Book' section. They have left it too late, are on the pension, and have failed to provide a comfortable, financially secure future for themselves. They struggle every day and there is not a thing they can do about it. Banks may not lend them money, and there is no hope of a better financial future. They just exist. Crosswords and bingo activities are all they can afford. A highlight of their year is the retirement village Christmas party. They may be very happy, they may consist of the 'coulda, woulda, shoulda' group, or they are just blissfully unaware that they could have or should have done more for themselves or for a legacy for their family.

Succeeded: They have a big house, an excellent portfolio, and they have steady income. They are self-funded retirees who do not need more investments.

It is important to note that these stereotypes do not prevent someone from changing or evolving. They do not restrict someone's attitude from changing.

CHAPTER 2

100K Plan (Your Personal Concierge)

Most people fail to invest for their future; many try, but do not try hard enough or stick it out. A plan, consisting of appropriate strategies for your personal situation and goals, is fundamental to improving the outcome of investing in property. You need to have a purpose. It is not enough to research a state, suburb, or property prior to purchasing if the property is in isolation to a short- and long-term plan. The property may perform well, but what then? What do you do with it?

Making unplanned, emotional, and ad hoc decisions leads to failure. You need to be proactive, not reactive. You are unique, and deserve a personalised, tailored approach, not just one off the rack.

Ultimately, the goal of the plan is to ensure you live comfortably in retirement, but also provide you the choice as to when you retire. A portfolio can be designed to work for you. If your portfolio is your personal 'bank,' you can deposit certain properties into your 'bank' that can be cashed in later on or leveraged off: blocks of land subdivided, more dwellings built on the land, more income streams, or more growth manufactured. But before that, the same properties can provide you growth and income to feed reality into your dreams.

Do not buy haphazardly; it is riskier to not have direction and focus. You need to be diversified to spread risk and enhance potential.

Potential is not just capital growth from your properties, it is also your borrowing capacity with a lender.

A plan always starts with the end in mind, so you can then map out what needs to be done. This should be tied back to what your circumstances are in order to correlate your situation with the desired outcome, which can determine if your desired outcome is realistic. If it is not, a plan can still help you achieve a much better outcome than no plan. It can help you follow a path parallel to the plan and follow the appropriate strategies to get you closer to where you want to be.

Your financial capacity leads to your borrowing capacity and affordability. You need credit worthiness to get a pre-approval and maintain a buffer (not just in borrowing capacity, but also in savings/equity). Assess these factors in order to recommend your next course of action.

Determine whether you wish to borrow 80% or more, and weigh up the benefit of LMI (Lenders Mortgage Insurance), principal and interest or interest-only repayments, ownership structure, and entity for tax benefits and asset protection (the two are generally mutually exclusive).

Goals

Choose a date to aim for and a dollar figure you would like/need in retirement. Your goals can also include leaving a property portfolio as a legacy. Your age will influence the time frame. If you are fifty-five years of age, you may only have fifteen years until retirement, whereas if you are thirty-five, your strategy could be vastly different as time is on your side. Your risk appetite will also influence the time needed for an outcome. If you have a more aggressive approach, an outcome could potentially be achieved quicker, but with more risk.

If you are more conservative, you may need more time in the market owning the properties for them to grow in value.

Ultimately, from a financial perspective, what matters is income. There is no point being asset rich and cash poor. Of course, you could sell off assets to provide cash to live off. This is okay, as you could potentially live off the asset equity if you have a loan set up with redraw or can get a loan against the properties, but the older you get, the harder it will be to get a loan. Cash flow is king.

Risk Profile and Appetite

Remember that your risk profile, when developing a property plan, is largely not used to determine if you should invest in property or if property is better than another kind of investment. Each type of strategy, location, and property has its own risks and benefits. Your risk profile can be used to assist with choosing a strategy and property more suited to you.

Surplus Income

This is if you have spare funds that you can put aside each week towards affording the cost of an investment property. Not many properties are positively geared, and if they are promoted as being positively geared, I would be wary as unexpected costs can occur. It is possible – if nothing is broken down or needs replacing or fixing, you had no vacancy, and interest rates did not rise – for a property to be positively geared, but let's face it, this is rarely the reality.

Investors may often over- or under-analyse, procrastinate, buy in the wrong area, or move too quickly due to their own procrastination. They may justify not doing enough due diligence as they see it as a positive step forward in overcoming their past procrastination. They often trust the wrong sales agent, buy the wrong type of property for the area, or buy in the wrong location, like a mining town or a one-horse town. They waste too much time looking at real estate pictures online and driving around. They may lack negotiation experience or do not know what to do at an auction. Perhaps they do not know how to interpret data, or they do not know what is good and bad in a purchase contract.

Too many investors think they know enough having gone to seminars, writing copious notes from meetings with different buyer's agents, and reading books. They purchase in the wrong position in the street, or in the wrong street entirely, after not getting independent advice, or not getting a property inspection. They often listen to family or friends that have little experience, and look at just one or two properties.

It would be too easy, and very wrong to base a decision on just one property. There are several considerations to bear in mind. Besides your exposure to the future cost of debt and receiving tax deductions, affordability to purchase more properties – whilst enabling you to continue to reduce your mortgage on your home – is very important. Combined, they provide hope; hope towards a brighter retirement, having done something rather than nothing.

An intelligent investor will not just focus on capital growth. They want to avoid the risk of becoming a slave to their portfolio, where they have to keep working just to make repayments and hoping they will wake up in ten years and the portfolio will have doubled in value. They want to sleep at night as interest rates rise (which they are, and will continue to independently of the Reserve Bank of Australia/RBA). An intelligent investor will not focus just on positive cash flow either, as they want to achieve capital growth and more wealth at retirement. Whilst they do not want their properties to be a negative impact on their current lifestyle, they realise the importance of capital growth.

Good capital growth locations typically have low yield. This would mean the property would likely be negatively geared. Cash flow is generally important to maintain affordability, manage holding costs, borrow more, and improve ability to grow a portfolio. Equity is equally important, as without it there is less money for deposit and costs. The power of leverage can provide considerable wealth. In general, it is not necessary to purchase ten averagely purchased properties when five to seven good ones may achieve the same result.

Cash flow focused properties are often in areas with less capital growth. At least this strategy reduces the risk of being exposed too much to the unknown future cost of debt. Fixing your interest rates can help as well, providing knowledge of what your repayments will be for a while. But no one can beat the banks – in the long term, it works out to roughly the same as having a variable rate loan.

People need help to invest in a practical way that suits them and their specific needs, not an ideological single strategy, bereft of suitability and sustainability to them.

Cash flow properties are not necessarily wealth creation properties. They do, however, provide greater income while you are growing your portfolio, therefore allowing a property investor an increased capacity to continue to borrow. If the focus is only on capital growth properties, the ability to continue to borrow money will diminish. Ultimately, the investor would run out of income to service the loans. If an investor could no longer borrow money, it would not matter how much equity they have, as they would be unable to access it.

Cash flow strategy: if you purchase in a further out or regional location, there can often be less amenities, infrastructure, growth, demand, potentially more supply or more land, and lower socio-demographic. Some people are naive; they think you should avoid positive cash flow because you pay more tax, but if you pay more tax in this case, it is because you are earning more. Isn't better to earn more? The positive cash flow nature of a property is often achieved only after tax deductions are taken into account.

The benefits of cash flow properties are lower holding costs and improved borrowing capacity which improves your ability to build a portfolio, lessens the negative impact on lifestyle, and helps protect you when rates rise. Any vacancy can be better absorbed. They are not always in regional areas; they could be a dual occupancy in a metro area of a capital city, or three townhouses on a block. The cons are that these properties have lower net worth eventually, and less growth.

Look for intrinsic growth drivers. The past is not an indication of the future, but it can be a great idea to buy where there has been performance. It is necessary to take this into account, but the location may be at the peak of its cycle and too late for you, so be careful. There may be intrinsic drivers to push growth along, or there could be a suburb next door that has not seen the same growth. Numbers are important, but appeal is also crucial for resale to a wider demographic.

It is important to appreciate and accept a balance between growth and yield. Yield is important to not weigh the buyer down in their living standard, while growth is important for wealth creation. Higher yield can be a great insurance policy in a rising rate market or in the accumulation and holding stage of an investment strategy.

A capital growth focused approach to property investment often has a less positive effect on improving a buyers' borrowing capacity from a servicing perspective, as capital growth properties generally provide less yield. However, a capital growth focused approach will often have greater potential to achieve more capital growth than buying a positive cash flow focused property. This benefit can provide more potential upswing in the equity of a property, equity that can be tapped into by successfully applying for a loan increase on the property. The problem with only using a capital growth investment strategy is that the investor becomes a slave to negative gearing and lifestyle sacrifices. They must keep working.

Results from property investment will vary and it is not possible to know for sure the percentage returns in the future. No one does. All one can do is undertake reasonable research, try to buy well, model more conservative returns in order to manage expectations, and, most of all, hold the investment for as long as possible (preferably fifteen to twenty years).

A portfolio generating income stems from capital growth as well as yield focused strategies. Wealth is through growth not yield alone, but wealth cannot be accumulated if you cannot afford to buy and hold the assets. It is important to be aware that if you find a good cash flow focused property, and you reduce the debt against it with your own income (either by making additional repayments or applying for principal and interest repayments on it), the property can make more positive cash flow, providing a passive income. The sooner people start making a passive income, the sooner they have greater choices.

For some, investing in second hand (established) properties is appealing. For others, it is less appealing than 'new' properties, from a holding cost, future cost desirability, and tax saving point of view. The important message here is that both capital growth and yield are proven wealth-building strategies, so there are opportunities for all types of investors to achieve their financial goals if they invest for the long term.

In April 2016, J.P. Morgan revealed in the *Australian Mortgage Industry Report* that finance for more property purchases was no longer possible for up to 10% of 'would be' investors. Lenders used to account for borrowers' existing debt with other lenders by using actual repayments to determine the borrowers' cost of debt. On an interest-only loan of 500K in 2016, the repayments might have been $22,500 p.a. Now, lenders are adding a buffer on top of the borrowing capacity calculator, and converting the interest-only repayments to a figure based on principal and interest, as they always have done for the new loan being applied for. The same 500K debt in 2017 would have a cost associated to it of $41,500 p.a., based not just on a higher qualifying rate, but also principal and interest repayments, even though the investor may be paying interest-only. This is $19,000 more income the borrowers need to afford the same debt on a lender's calculator as they previously could have. Imagine if they only purchased capital growth properties and none of them were cash flow focused properties. This investor would be in strife, and on two main fronts.

1. *Not being able to borrow as much*

   and/or

2. *Being forced to sell one or more properties, due to rising rates and holding cost of debt.*

Many investors over the years have been drawn to negative gearing, yet it makes less sense why. They think they are saving a great deal of tax, but let's put this into perspective. According to the ATO, over 70% of investors that have a negatively geared property (a property not breaking even or not making positive cash flow) earn under 80K per annum. So, their tax bracket is mid-range, not high. It is really foolish to spend a dollar just to save 32.5 cents, which is what *all* these people are doing. This is only okay if the property makes enough capital growth, the tax savings are large enough to justify the expense, and the investor does not have to make any unreasonable sacrifices to their lifestyle.

The other risk many investors take is that they will, at some point in the near future, struggle with carrying these losses through the year. This risk may be made more bearable if they have filled in the required variation form (more on this in my previous book, *Property Finance Made Simple*).

There are three overarching portfolio growth strategies for property investors; capital growth and cash flow strategies can be implemented in all three. The difference between the three of them is the level of risk, time available to retirement, your tailored plan, comfort level, and various other influences.

- ### Buy and Hold

This is perhaps the easiest of the three strategies. It is more suited to time poor investors who wish to be a little more conservative, or who lack the knowledge and expertise to risk undertaking one of the other two strategies. Buy and hold is what the majority of investors decide on. Many still fail for innumerable reasons, such as lack of knowledge and experience, poor research, not using an advisor, bad financial strategy, having no plan, selling too early, buying at the wrong time in the wrong market, or buying the wrong property type in a good suburb.

- ***Flipping or Holding by Renovating***

This requires a more hands-on approach or paying a premium to have someone renovate for you. The purchaser can manufacture more capital growth and cash flow independently of the market, so they are not solely reliant on the market for the property's performance. If too much emotion is involved and they over-capitalise, serious problems will arise. Having the property vacant for an extended period while work is being carried out means you will be out of pocket for a period of time. Affordability could then be an issue, as it is more difficult to afford to have a property vacant for an extended period.

- ***Develop***

This includes construction of another dwelling or several dwellings on the block, and/or subdivision. This is the riskiest strategy, due to time and cost, but it has the potential for significantly more financial benefits from a cash flow and capital growth perspective. A feasibility study would be required to determine if the project will make enough money or will lose money. You will also need a good team around you. Refer to www.propertyinvestingmadesimple.com.au to get an idea of who would be needed in your team for this type of investment. Also, my next book, *Commercial Property and Residential Development Made Simple,* goes into significant detail on everything to do with small-scale developments.

There are Three Stages with Every Plan

1. An Acquisition Phase

This is the period of time over which you acquire the required properties. It can be as short or long as is practical, but it needs to suit your current situation and all the elements of what makes up your current situation (as were discussed in Chapter 1).

2. The Holding Phase

This is the period of time that you hold your properties. The longer this phase, the more time the properties have to grow in value. Many property marketing companies will tell you that property has doubled in value every seven to ten years. Whilst this is true in many areas, what these people often do wrong is they imply that property will continue to double the next seven to ten years. This I disagree with. The past is not a reliable indicator of the future. To be more reasonable in order to manage expectations, it is more sensible to allow fifteen years, or even twenty.

Not everyone has this much time, and it is a sad fact that people leave it too late in life to take action for the betterment of their future. What can be done, for people who are young enough, is to consider starting now if your current situation allows it. For those people who have left it late, they could also consider whether they should start now to at least try and improve their situation, and seek advice at least. The older someone becomes, the more conservative they should consider being. They have less time to try and mitigate any financial mistakes they make.

3. Exit Phase

There are five main exit strategies. It is best to seek advice from a property advisor for a tailored approach.

1. *Sell some properties and pay off the debt on the rest, leaving the remaining properties hopefully unencumbered. This works when there are more than just a few properties, and some with a capital growth focus. You may or may not have reduced some of the debt. The less debt you want to reduce, the more confidence you would need with the market.*

2. *Reduce your debt, assisted by an offset account and principal and interest (P&I) repayments on any mortgage against your principal place of residence (PPR). Firstly, focus on the debt not providing any tax benefit. Once non- deductible debt is paid off, then consider an offset against any deductible debt against the principal place of residence (PPR) stemming from using equity in your PPR toward the deposit and costs of acquiring your Investment property, or, if you don't have any debt against your PPR, consider an offset account against any debt against your investment property.*

3. *A blend of Strategy 1 and Strategy 2 is optimal, unless all debt can be paid off from personal endeavour (e.g. working for a living).*

4. *Live off equity in retirement. Prior to retiring, apply to refinance all properties, setting up redraw or line of credit against some or all. Using equity, after any capital gains tax has been paid, to live off is different to earning income to live off, as equity is not taxed as income would be.*

5. *Sell all properties, then purchase a few properties with very high yield (for example, 10%) and live off the rent.*

Example: If your home, or preferably an investment property, had enough equity to establish a cash out/equity release amount to sit in redraw of 400K just before retirement, while still earning assumedly sufficient income to service this amount, the undrawn equity could sit in the loan not incurring interest. It could provide 40K p.a. to live off for ten years, which would put the borrower in the top percentage of retired income earners in Australia. Let's assume superannuation and any additional shares provide an income of 15K p.a. Only 25K needs to be used from the line of credit/redraw to earn 40K per year, meaning the 400K in redraw could last for sixteen years. Imagine having a couple of properties with access to 400K equity in each.

Note: Strategy 4 is one that some professionals promote. It has, as a concept, been around for twenty years, but often these people fail to adequately explain the mechanics and downside of it.

Some reasons it may be problematic are:

- *Accessing equity after retirement is very difficult and unlikely, as lenders will need the borrower to have enough income to service an increase in the existing debt level, and an acceptable exit strategy.*
- *Lending policy may inhibit further borrowing; you cannot rely on what lenders will do in five or twenty-five years. Additionally, it is not always so easy to refinance just because the borrower wants to.*
- *You will eventually die, potentially leaving all the debt-covered properties to someone else. This would be unfortunate and not considered a welcome legacy.*
- *Some elderly people decide on a reverse mortgage, and this does have serious consequences. It is one of the most expensive forms of debt, may leave the person unable to afford aged care, and it may affect pension eligibility.*

Summary

The type of property strategy and the number of properties utilising each strategy will impact on the investor's suburb location choice. Between five to seven well-purchased properties is better than just choosing a number as a naïve goal for a portfolio. Property advisors have software to model outcomes, and they should be using conservative assumptions of growth and yield figures.

It is important that investors do not just buy and then sit and wait. They need to review their plan, portfolio, and goals based on any changes to their circumstances, the performance of the property, and the market which it is in. Using conservative figures will manage your expectations. It means that if the portfolio performs better, you may exceed the income you had planned for. If it does not perform as well as you might anticipate, at least you have been conservative.

Reducing debt that provides tax deductions is not necessarily the best approach. This type of debt does have other benefits, which need to be weighed up. Whilst any applicable depreciation on the dwelling, subject to applicable legislation, is on a straight-line method at 2.5% each year over forty years, depreciation on fittings and fixtures, if applicable, does diminish over the short term, so the cost of debt will increase accordingly.

Note: The Government eliminated the ability for investors to claim depreciation on fittings and fixtures that came with the property, as of June 2017. To help mitigate the potential higher holding cost of owning an investment property due to less tax deductions associated with no longer being able to claim depreciation on fixtures and fittings that came with the property, (and to help weather the storm of rising rates) – especially on interest-only and investment loans to maximum the difference between the value of the property and level of debt, and make it more cash flow positive (if you can afford to) – a debt reduction strategy can generally be considered wise.

The bigger picture is the focus here. If you significantly reduce your debt over time, it will lessen the debt against your properties and perhaps reduce the number of properties you need to sell. It is very important to consider principal and interest repayments on the properties.

You need capital growth for wealth creation. This can provide the equity which may be accessed to use for the deposit and costs of buying more properties, and paying off debt on other properties nearer to retirement, leaving a final number unencumbered. Paul Clitheroe from *Money Magazine* (2018) proposes a multiple of 17. Work out what income/savings you need in retirement, and then multiply it by 17. He suggests that 17 is the number of years you will live beyond retirement. If you live beyond that, or if you retire too early, then you may be in trouble.

A plan's focus is to acquire an appropriate number of properties for your specific needs, over a given time at a given price, and to achieve a desired passive income all within an appropriate risk tolerance and level of affordability.

Within a plan, there are several further considerations that must be included. Invest within your risk profile and regularly review your portfolio performance, your circumstances, and the market to ensure that your goals are more likely to be achieved.

Have a contingency fund for property expenses to give you peace of mind should something go wrong. I recommend three to six months' equivalent of rent. This can be in a redraw facility, for example. Funds required for a healthy contingency fund are generally three months' worth of rent for all investment property costs.

Consider any applicable insurances:

- *Body corporate insurance, when required, covers the building replacement only. All internal fixtures and fittings need to be insured at the owner's cost. If you are buying property without a body corporate (or even sometimes with), you will be responsible for the building insurance as well as fixtures and fittings (contents).*
- *Maintain landlord insurance to protect your rental income and property from rogue tenants, accidents, and other unfortunate situations. Building and landlord insurance may start from $800 p.a.*
- *Title insurance could be important when buying any property, either new or established. This insurance can protect the buyer in a number of ways from situations such as:*
    - Illegal building works/extensions or conversions
    - Title or planning issues
    - Identity theft/fraud
    - Boundary issues
    - Any rates and taxes that you, the buyer, may inherit

The fee could be from $400 upward, as a one-off fee, depending on the value of the property.

- *It is important to remember that if circumstances change due to illness, change of employment, or anything else significant, that your plan should be revisited to try and optimise it.*
- *Investors chasing growth properties require more surplus household cash flow to meet the shortfall between the rental income and the cost of holding the property.*
- *A yield strategy usually means the cost of holding a property is much lower, so less surplus cash flow is required. It can be a good option for households who do not have a strong cash flow surplus or for whom surplus cash flows are likely to be impacted in the future.*
- *By opting for a yield strategy, more 'would be' investors could get their investment property journey underway.*

Gearing

A strategy will never include negative gearing as an intentional focus, as this is simply a by-product of a property purchase that is not cash flow positive. It is more commonly referred to as a by-product of capital growth. To build a portfolio, people are wrong to think they should choose to avoid or include negative gearing in their plan. The correct question is how best to move forward in an affordable manner?

Your LVR (Loan to Value Ratio) – more specifically, your level of debt and the cost of that debt versus income coming in from the property – will determine if the property is negatively geared. Any property can end up being positively geared; it depends on how much money you pay towards it versus how much money you borrow for the property.

Whether you are starting out, midway through your life, or further you continually need to assess your options of how geared you wish to be. Starting out on your journey may require you to borrow a higher amount and, in turn, incur a higher LMI premium, as you may not have much saved or not have accumulated any capital growth in your assets. Later, as your portfolio grows, provided you do things properly, you will more likely have realised some capital growth and, eventually, you should become less geared.

Seek advice from a suitably qualified professional. Salespeople from property marketing companies are not the professionals I refer to, nor are real estate agents. They are not in the arena of providing independent, unbiased advice to buyers if they are acting for a seller in the same transaction. Someone who is qualified and fully licensed as a real estate agent and experienced as a buyer's agent, but who is not in the business of marketing or selling property, is of immense value to have in your team of professionals. They possess the same education as a fully licensed sales agent, and you can leverage off that. At the same time, they are unbiased in their assistance to you.

Whilst creating the plan, and engaging the services of a good advisory firm, the advisor you employ can work with you to improve your borrowing capacity via the choice of properties. It is important to manage your spending during the plan to lessen the risk of any financial difficulty. Always have a buffer, continually reassess your lending/financial/property strategy in order to continue to correlate and enhance your tailored plan.

A portfolio should be designed to be as bulletproof as possible to withstand different cycles, economic turmoil, and consumer sentiment changes. Understand your goal and your risk appetite (which is shaped from attitudinal and experiential outlook), but also your income, job security, and budget.

Budget forms two key foundations of property investment:

- *Your borrowing capacity with a lender*
- *Your surplus income*

Investing in blue chip areas close to the CBDs of the Eastern Seaboard is important for capital growth. However, if interest rates rise, you lose your job, or your budget gets a bit tight, you may need a defensive strategy by way of positive cash flow to help protect you and your interests.

Rentvesting

This section is not just for people who own a home or have a mortgage on a property they live in; it is also for people currently renting, who want to get into the property market. Continuing to rent whilst investing provides a greater ability to get into the market. It sets the investor on the way to creating wealth, while allowing more freedom and flexibility to rent in an area where the investor could not normally afford to buy.

The greater ability I refer to is related to your borrowing capacity with a lender. If you buy an investment property, a bank will generally factor in rental income to help with servicing the debt and add back the cost of interest repayments on the debt. They would be considered a tax deduction, which also helps with improving borrowing capacity. Neither of these two factors will be used when buying a principal place of residence.

Hopefully, the investor has been smart enough to avoid paying an excessive amount of rent just to live in a certain postcode, given the more rent you pay, the more out of pocket cost. It negatively impacts on the investor's ability to borrow for an investment property. When someone rents, the landlord pays the insurance, electricity and gas rates, water rates, body corporate fees (if any), property maintenance fees, council rates, and for general upkeep. The tenant can therefore save more money to invest, compared to living in a property where they have a mortgage against the title.

Any good mortgage broker should be able to spell out just how much easier it is to buy an investment property than a home. An owner-occupied mortgage or mortgage for the purpose of buying a property to live in is often referred to as 'bad' debt; it provides no tax deductions, must be paid entirely out of the owner's pocket, and has no rent coming in to assist.

A home loan debt will also have a dramatically negative impact on the investor's ability to borrow, compared to borrowing money for an investment property. At least with an investment, there may be tax deductions and there is most likely rent coming in from a tenant to assist with the cost of holding the property. If an investment property is ready for a tenant, but it is vacant, it would be due to a number of things.

1. *Owner's choice. For example, perhaps they are from an overseas country, such as China, and do not care about rental income.*

2. *It was purchased in a less desirable suburb and/or area within the suburb. For example, it is on the wrong street, near negative infrastructure like a major road, under high tension power lines, near a prison or an industrial area, or under a flight path of an airport.*

3. *The owner is asking too much rent and tenants are not interested.*

Investment debt is often referred to as 'good' debt, as it can provide tax deductions. Interest rates matter less on deductible debt compared to non-deductable debt, as tax deductions and the treatment of rising costs of interest repayments on a lenders' borrowing capacity calculator could have a positive impact (albeit slightly) toward your borrowing capacity.

In a rising interest rate market, rent may also trend upwards, aided by buying well in an area where the average income is increasing and there is favourable balance of demand versus supply.

The upshot to this is that instead of focusing on the difficulties of first-home buyers, who often struggle to get a toehold in the market, perhaps you should be considering property investment as a way to get your foot in the door to start with. That way, if you feel compelled to buy a home of your own when children arrive on the scene, you have hopefully already created enough equity in your investments for a deposit on the property you desire.

Property Advice Model

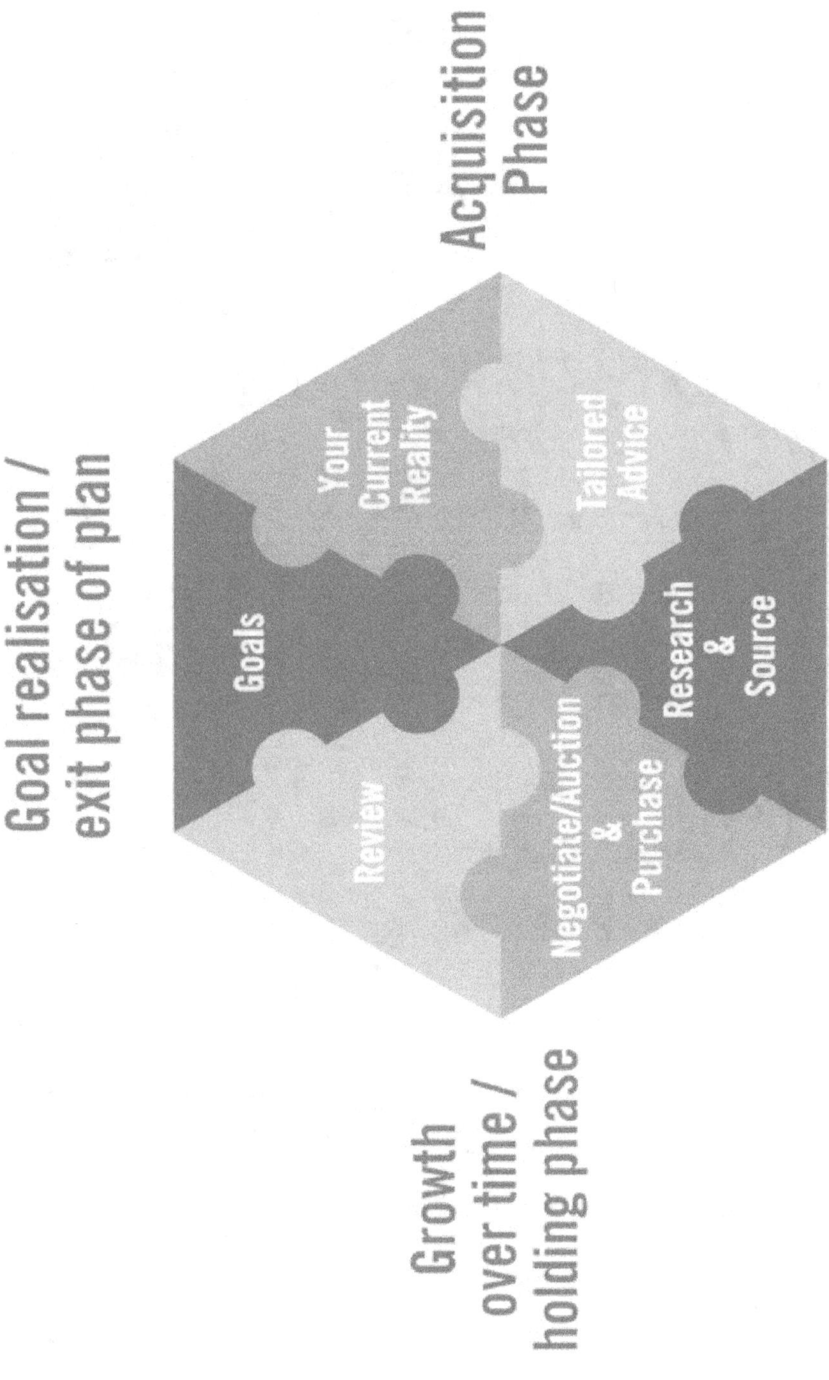

Goals

- Start with your goals and work backwards
- Determine passive income
- Desired exit strategy and phase
- Realise the outcome
- Monitor proximity to your goals as we progress

Your Current Reality

- Assets, liabilities
- Income
- Surplus income
- Risk appetite and profile
- Full 'fact find'
- Needs, wants, desires

Tailored Advice

- An individualised plan of where, what and when to buy
- Education on risks & benefits
- Risk reduction
- Improved potential
- Due diligence
- Buyers best interest model

Research & Source

- Research suburbs with capital growth, cash flow potential or both
- This includes any state in Australia
- All types of property considered depending on what suits you: New; (house & land, off the plan or completed), established, house, townhouse, unit, duplex, dual occupancy, regional, inner city, positive cash flow, capital growth
- Model holding costs, income & considerations

Negotiate / Auction & Purchase

- Acquire the property at the best price possible
- Locate property managers, quantity surveyors, insurance providers, property & pest inspectors, mortgage brokers & conveyance firms
- Develop the team around you

Review

- Review your plan & tweak where necessary
- Ongoing assessment of property, suburb performance & yield
- Review performance of property manager
- Continued implementation of the plan

Scenario

This is a scenario which is familiar to many Australians at a similar age.

Our clients Laura and Matteo are wanting to invest in property. I ran a scenario with the intention of having a 100K p.a. income in retirement. I have modelled four properties being purchased.

General Information

- *Married couple, Matteo and Laura, both aged 45*
- *Two children, aged 16 and 10*
- *Matteo earns an income of $100,000 p.a.*
- *Laura earns an income of $50,000 p.a.*
- *Living expenses of $78,000 p.a.*
- *Principal residence valued at $900,000*
- *Principal residence mortgage of $300,000, interest rate of 4.5% p.a., 15-year term remaining*
- *Offset account of $100,000, income rate of 1.5% p.a. once loan is repaid.*
- *Both Matteo and Laura retire at age 65.*

Strategy: Purchase Four Investment Properties

In Year One, the couple purchase their first property.

- *Investment Property 1 (cash flow property):*
- *Purchased at the start of Year One for $550,000 with purchase* costs of $35,000.
- Establish five-year interest-only loan for $585,000 at a rate of 5% p.a. (note: it is 100% financed, with part of the loan against the investment property, and part against the principle place of residence).

- Income rate (yield) of 5.5% p.a. and capital *growth of 3.5% p.a.*
- *Ongoing deductible expenses of 1% p.a.*

In Year Two, the couple purchase their second property.

- *Investment Property 2 (growth property):*
- *Purchased at the start of Year Two for $600,000 with purchase costs of $37,500.*
- *Establish five-year interest-only loan for $637,500 at a rate of 5% p.a. (note: it is 100% financed, with part of the loan against the investment property, and part against the principle place of residence).*
- *Income rate (yield) of 3.5% p.a. and capital growth of 5.5% p.a.*
- *Ongoing deductible expenses of 1% p.a.*

In between buying the second and third property, Matteo and Laura accumulate savings in their offset account.

In Year Five, the couple purchase their third property.

- *Investment Property 3 (cash flow property):*
- *Purchased at the start of Year Five for $700,000 with purchase costs of $44,000.*
- *Establish five-year interest-only loan for $744,000 at a rate of 5% p.a. (note: it is 100% financed, with part of the loan against the investment property, and part against the principle place of residence).*
- *Income rate (yield) of 5.5% p.a. and capital growth of 3.5% p.a.*
- *Ongoing deductible expenses of 1% p.a.*

In Year Six, the couple purchase their fourth property

- *Investment Property 4 (growth property):*

- *Purchased at the start of Year Six for $750,000 with purchase costs of $47,000.*
- *Establish five-year interest-only loan for $797,000 at a rate of 5% p.a. (note: it is 100% financed, with part of the loan against the investment property, and part against the principle place of residence).*
- *Income rate (yield) of 3.5% p.a. and capital growth of 5.5% p.a.*
- *Ongoing deductible expenses of 1% p.a.*
- *When each interest-only loan expires after five years, the loan is restructured as a thirty-year principal and interest loan.*
- *Once their home loan is fully paid off or their offset account reaches a balance of $300,000 (offsetting their $300,000 mortgage) cash flow freed up from not having to make repayments on the $300,000 is used to make additional repayments on the investment debt.*

Upon Retirement at Age 65:

- *They sell Investment Property 4 and use the net proceeds (after accounting for sales costs of 2%) to repay debt.*
- *Direct any surplus cash flow:*
    - To further reducing debt.
- *Direct any capital gains to:*
    - The repayment of debt.

Cash Flow Outcomes

- *Provides sufficient cash flow to meet all property holding and living expenses*

<u>At Age 65</u>

- *Incurs capital gains tax of $1,654,000 up to this point*

At Age 85

- *Tax of $3,471,000 up to this point*

Net Worth Outcomes

At Age 65

- *Assets of $9,558,000 and liabilities of $1,608,000 – calculated to a net worth of $7,950,000 or $4,323,000 net present value.* (Please refer to Figure 1)

Liabilities

- *Have debts fully repaid by age 67. So holding assets to age 85 is naturally acceptable, as they provide income and they won't have debt against them, and they can be bequeathed as a legacy to family.*

At Age 85

- *Has assets of $18,516,000 and liabilities of $0 – having a net worth of $18,516,000 or $5,311,000 net present value.* (Please refer to Figure 2)

You can see that the longer the strategy runs, the more beneficial the holding assets.

This strategy should be done once a risk profile is completed (upon advice sought). Buying property has been shown as a great way of increasing your wealth. However, if there should be a period of ill health and one partner cannot work due to illness or an accident, the whole strategy could put the couple in a much worse position. A full suite of insurances should be considered as a safeguard and a way of ensuring the strategies can be successful.

This strategy works because of the equity in the home, the ability to borrow against the home and each property, negative gearing, and the ability to offset interest paid against the income of both Matteo and Laura. This strategy uses interest-only repayments to start with to assist cash flow, while the rent is doing a great job towards covering the interest payments.

Figure 1

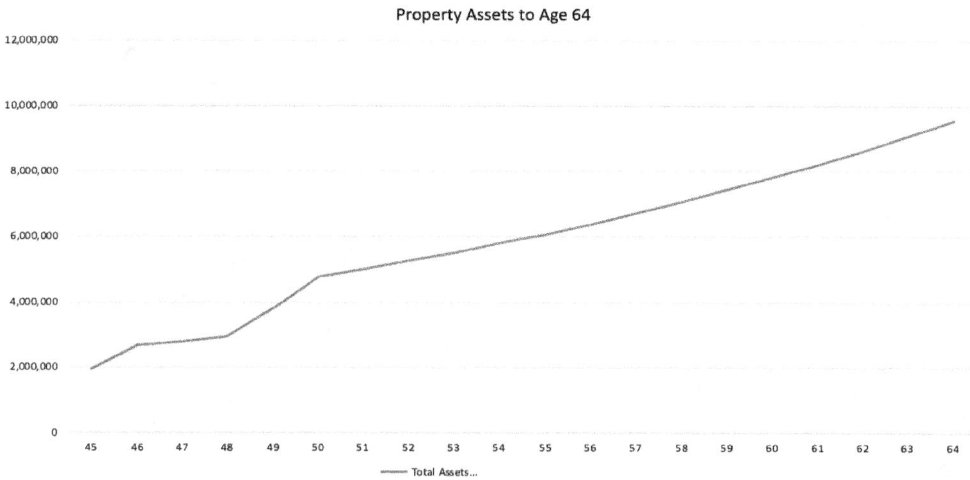

Figure 2

Figure 3

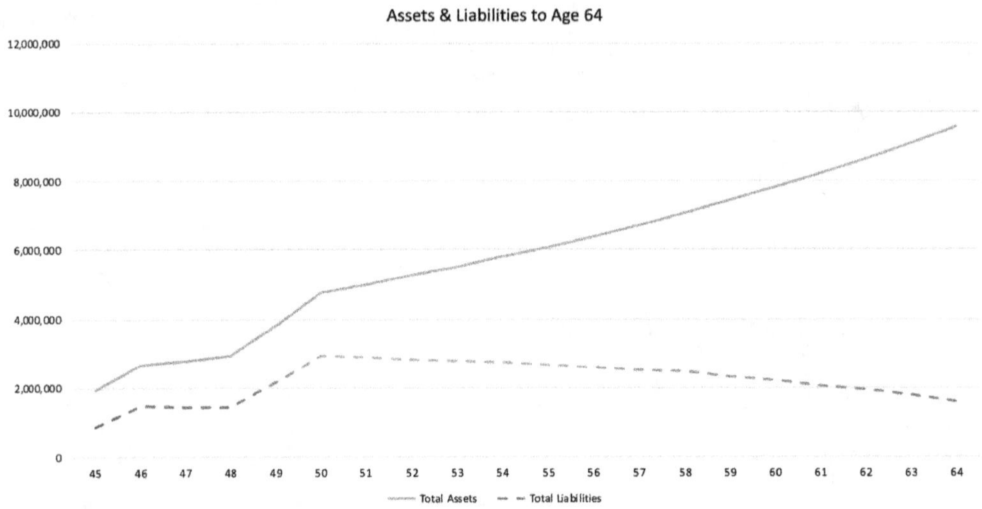

Figure 4

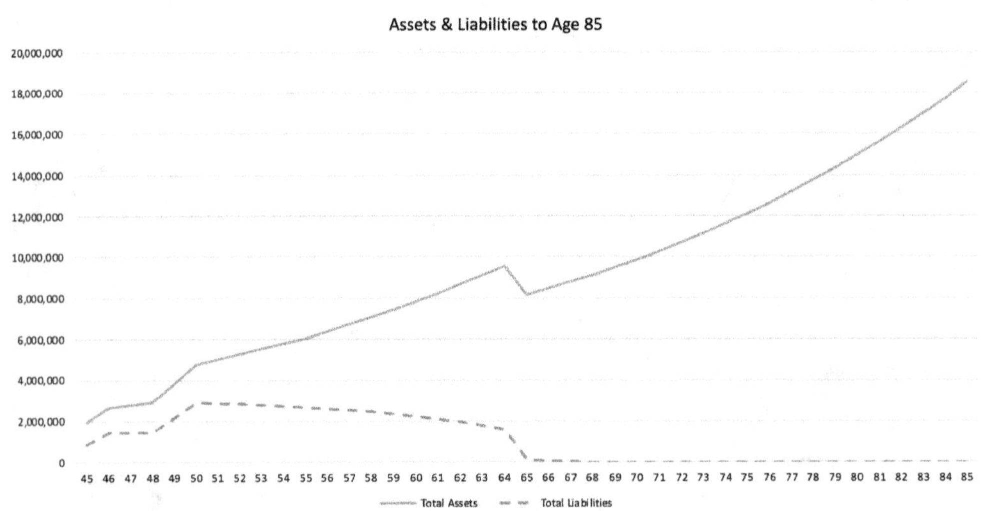

Figure 5: Cash Flow

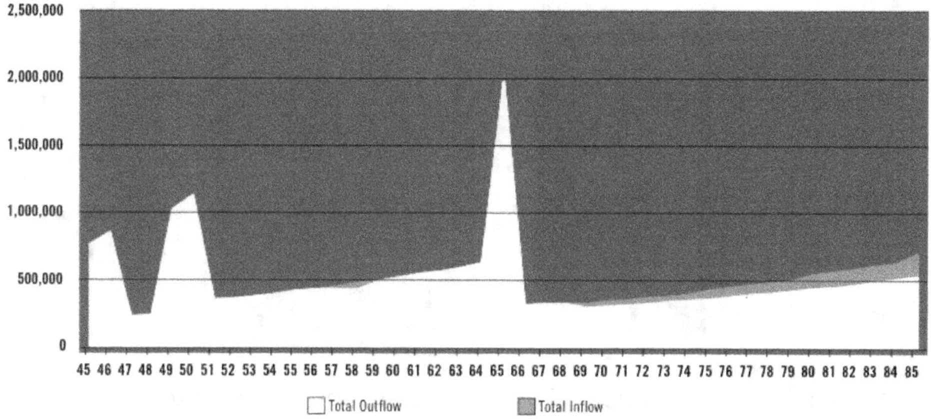

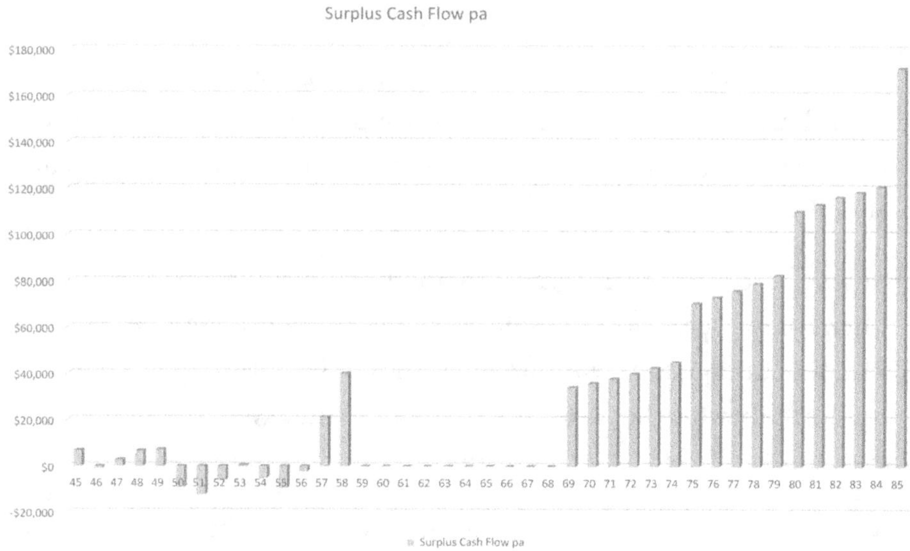

In conclusion, in this scenario and example, a couple of this age (with a household income that is generally accepted as being reasonable) will earn $100,000 a year from just four properties. In the cash flow graph, you can see the income generated from the portfolio.

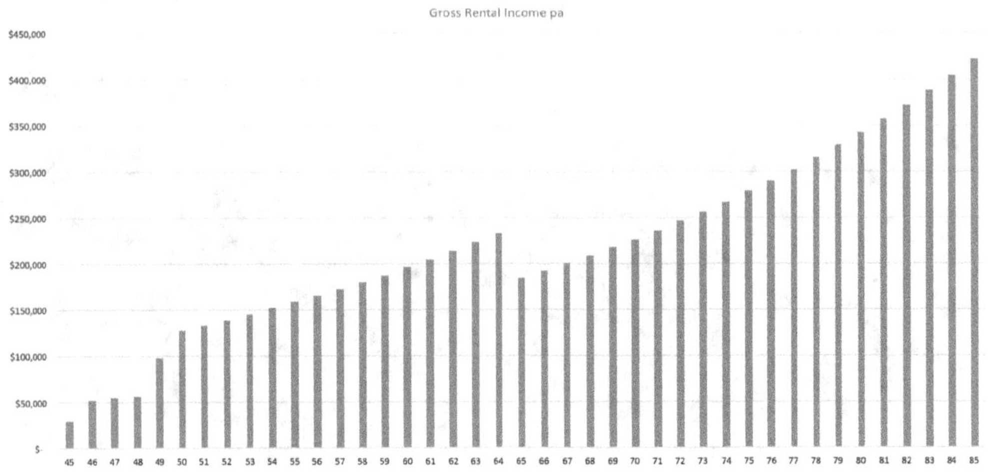

At age 64, the 4th property is sold. This essentially provides enough equity to pay off all their other loans, leaving them debt free. Their income is far exceeding $100,000 p.a.

In fact, it is approximately $175,000 taxable income and it goes up from there. From this income, they pay property holding expenses – such as rates, insurance, and any maintenance – and they live can live off it.

Note: this combined income is actually higher than their income when they were working for a living. In retirement a couple, without children, and with no debt, should be able to survive more comfortably with the same level of income they were earning when they had dependents and a mortgage.

Now, for those investors who listen to other advice, and perhaps just continue with interest-only loans until they retire, (not so easy anymore with lenders appetites and borrowing capacity calculator changes) their debt levels would be much higher, the cost of the debt over the length of the plan will be much higher, and selling more than one property would be necessary, leading to less income being available in retirement.

I believe that ideally it is not worth relying just on the market, but rather try to reduce debt over the life of the plan, so when it comes to retiring, you have more options. You will have less debt, it will be less of a problem if the market has not performed how you would have preferred, and you will have a greater amount of equity in the properties working for you.

The biggest mistake people make is having an interest-only loan for 5-10-15 years, then either refinancing to another 30-year loan term or, if they cannot refinance, the loan will revert to principle and interest with amortized repayments over 25-20-15 years depending on how long the interest-only period was of that loan. Consider how painful the extra repayments will be in a more condensed time period. It could be as much as double the interest-only repayments.

Without a plan, investors are doomed to fail. If an investor purchases each property in isolation to the other properties they own without the properties complementing each other by way of a balance between capital growth and cash flow, they will likely struggle.

It is most important to strike a balance between affording the debt now (deciding between interest-only and principle and interest), affording the debt in 5 years on principle and interest, and not being a slave to the debt you have.

Undertake thorough research, and if you don't have time, then pay someone to do it for you. Spending 10-15k on a buyer's agent to reduce the risk of making a 500k. to 1-million-dollar mistake is worth it.

Besides, having a buyer's agent negotiate for you, could save you the equivalent of their fee in the process.

CHAPTER 3

Finance

Get finance ready and improve your borrowing capacity.

In any property investment plan, the most important thing you need to know – besides what you can afford to borrow – is your financial strategy. A property plan can often involve a number of considerations, depending on the plan and the individual's circumstances. Until you know what you can borrow and, preferably, what the finance strategy may look like, you cannot start looking for a property, unless you want to waste your time.

The considerations could include:

1. *An order in which a lender is used in applying for finance. Far too often, I see borrowers haphazardly applying for a loan, not considering which lender's calculators work best for their circumstances, and only approaching the lenders who assess existing debt more favourably later on when some debt has been obtained.*

2. *Using a good broker. Anything less risks being myopically minded, foolhardy, and haphazard in its approach. 50% of the population fall into the category of going straight to a bank. Bank branches can place a great deal of pressure on their 'in house' loan writers, expecting them to cross-sell insurance, financial planning services, and other types of debt, like credit cards and personal loans. As*

recent events have demonstrated, even the biggest banks can be investigated for scandals, sell the wrong insurance products to the wrong people, and end up investigated by the regulatory authorities for alleged involvement in money laundering, fraud, corruption, charging fees to the deceased, and other illicit activities.

3. *Before applying for any loan, you must understand your budget and understand what you are really spending. Look through all your credit card and bank statements to remind yourself what annual or monthly fees are coming out. These could include gym memberships, Netflix or Foxtel subscriptions, PO boxes, annual fees for your loans, car insurance, rates, car registration, energy bills, mobile phone plans, LinkedIn premium membership, and toll road expenses.*

You have more control over some of these expenses than others. Rates, you cannot do anything about, nor registration of your vehicles. A lot of the rest you can shop around and compare for the best price. More cost of debt and living expenses means less borrowing capacity. The amount of debt you have may have less direct impact on your borrowing capacity than the cost of that debt.

Consider reducing your credit card limits, and simplifying your life to just one or two debts. Approaching your car loan provider, the ATO (if you have a tax debt), or your credit card provider to consolidate your debts, and comparing energy, insurance, and mobile and home phone providers can all have an impact.

Look at your unexpected expenses over the last two to three years, such as hot water system, fridge or washing machine replacement, new tyres for your car, property repairs and maintenance, holidays, the cost of your child's birthday party, rounds of drinks at the pub on a Friday night, lottery tickets, alcohol, cigarettes, medical and dental bills, prescriptions, subscriptions to newspapers and magazines, or school fees. Now, average it over twelve months, and break it down into a cost per month and week. This can help provide a more reliable buffer to maintain. It provides transparency of what is being spent and where certain costs can be discarded. It allows you to be more accountable to yourself (and your partner). These things can help improve your borrowing capacity.

The most important thing a borrower needs to consider is what the loan will cost them every month (repayment figure) and whether the loan is suitable or not suitable for their own needs. It should never be only about interest rate. 'Would be' borrowers must also consider (if they are currently renting) whether they should continue to rent, or whether they should 'buy to live in' rather than 'buy as investment.'

Loan Assessment

Always bear in mind the costs associated with buying an investment property. Lenders will need to see that you have the money to pay the difference between the loan amount and the purchase price plus costs. Costs can include stamp duty, conveyancer fees, lender costs (these could be application fees, legal costs, or sometimes valuation), and possibly lenders mortgage insurance.

Credit checks are done whenever you apply for a credit card, interest free terms on a lounge suite purchase or similar, and every time you apply for a loan. Applicants themselves are known to, somewhat inadvertently, create problems for themselves, such as by shopping around for the best rate. By making enquiries with different lenders, they can degrade the quality of their own credit history. Each time they shop around, a hit on their credit history may be generated. The more you do this, the more you are a danger to yourself. The danger is becoming less palatable to a lender. Use a broker to compare options for you.

Loan assessment can take a matter of hours or weeks, depending on the lender. Do not rely on an answer from a lender one day before you want to go to auction. Do not apply for finance after bidding at auction or entering into negotiations on a property; this is just mad. Always have a 'subject to finance' clause in a purchase contract, if you can. Remember, you cannot have this if you are successful at auction.

A proper pre-approval, as opposed to a conditional approval, is where the lender assesses everything to make you finance ready to find a property. Pre-approvals can be valid for 30 to 180 days. Ensure your finance clause does not expire prior to a valuation being done by the lender on the property.

Valuation can be computer generated or the valuer may want to visit the property. The lender will decide. This can take a few hours or over a week, and even longer if there are plans and permits in place on the property.

From formal approval to the documents stage, it can take a few hours to perhaps two days. Once documents are returned, the lender may normally require 24 to 48 hours to settle, unless there is a refinance involved. This can take more time, as the outgoing lender that you are refinancing away from can often drag their feet, conveniently making more money off your loan.

The time from submission of the loan to settlement can be as quick as a week, but normally it would take three to six weeks, depending on the lender.

To understand the requirements for submitting a loan application to obtain finance, please refer to my book *Property Finance Made Simple*.

Brokers

A good mortgage broker is vital, and I recommend using them for many reasons. One that stands out for anyone – whether you are an upsizer, downsizer, extender, refinancer, first-home buyer, first-time investor, or growing property investor – is that the broker can compare the borrowing capacity calculators of various lenders and the differing loan amounts you can borrow.

The broker can help you by packaging up the deal to sell it to the lender, working towards convincing them to lend money to you. Some borrowers need all the help they can get. It is not just a matter of giving the lender a bunch of statements and expecting a loan to be provided.

Good brokers do a lot of work behind the scenes on their loan submission notes to list the strengths of the loan and paint a picture to the lender. They chase the deal, pushing it through the process, plus they have the right contacts.

'Servicing' is a key factor that a lender focuses on when forming a decision on whether they want to approve a loan or continue saying "yes" to the applicant. The borrowing capacity will vary between lenders, as do policy, procedure, and product attributes. Brokers can compare many choices — a service that any one lender cannot offer you.

Another reason why I think using a good broker can be highly beneficial, besides saving the time in finding a lender suitable for your needs, is that they chase documents for you, and you may get a better deal due to their relationships with some of the lenders (sometimes even better than if you went direct).

A good broker is there to help you understand the loan documents, and they shop around for you without incurring credit hits on your credit file, before submitting your loan to the chosen lender.

Finding a broker that specialises in particular product or borrower types, such as first-home buyers, construction, commercial finance, property investors, or non-conforming loans increases the likelihood of being offered a product to more suitably fit with the borrower's needs.

Construction Loan

Construction loans apply to a house and land contract. Normally the borrower is expected to pay either 5% or 10% of the land value and 5–10% of the construction contract as a deposit.

After the deposit for each land and construction contract is paid, the difference between what the bank is providing and the deposit is contributed by the borrower in order to settle (officially own) the land.

So, for example, if the LVR is 80% against the property, then 20% and costs has come from equity in another property owned, cash, a gift, or even an unsecured loan. Part of this is made available at settlement of the land, and the other part will be transferred by the borrower to the builder for the first payment owed during the construction process (otherwise known as Stage 1 payment). Evidence of the contribution by the borrower for Stage 1 must be provided to the lender.

The lender requires the borrower to put their own money in prior to them releasing the approved loan towards relevant stage payments (normally five in total). When each stage is complete, the builder will send an invoice to the borrower, who then signs and authorises their lender to pay within seven days.

Here is an example of the construction process: I have used $250,000 as the purchase price for the land, with 5% of this being paid as a deposit. I have used $300,000 as the example for the price of the fixed price construction contract, with 5% deposit (sometimes this is 10%) then as construction occurs, the builder will invoice you for more money, hopefully you have signed a contract in line with HIA standards which dictate a fair % of money attributable to each stage of the build, as it is completed

Figure 6

LAND PRICE BASED ON $250,000	$
CONSTRUCTION $300,000	
Deposit	15,000
Stage 1 - Slab	30,000
Stage 2 - Frame	45,000
Stage 3 - Lock-up	105,000
Stage 4 - Fit-out	60,000
Stage 5 - Pract Comp	45,000

Refer to broker for loan structure

CONSTRUCTION CONTRACT: EXAMPLE ONLY

Based on 550k price (300k build and 250k land approx)

STAGE	TIME	PERCENTAGE OF BUILD PRICE	INTEREST EXPENSE PER MONTH		INTEREST EXPENSE AMOUNT REQUIRED UNTIL ANTICIPATED TENANCY
250k land price	month 1		(250,000 x 5% ÷ 12)	$1042.00	$8336.00
Deposit	month 1	5%	(15,000 x 5% ÷ 12)	$62.50	$500.00
Stage 1	month 2	10%	(30,000 x 5% ÷ 12)	$125.00	$875.00
Stage 2	month 2–3	15%	(45,000 x 5% ÷ 12)	$187.50	$1312.50
Stage 3	month 4	35%	(105,000 x 5% ÷ 12)	$437.50	$1750.00
Stage 4	month 5	20%	(60,000 x 5% ÷ 12)	$250.00	$750.00
Stage 5	month 6	15%	(45,000 x 5% ÷ 12)	$187.50	$375.00
STAMP DUTY	Stamp Duty based on 250k land (NSW)		$7,524.00		$13898.50 *

Handover approx 6–8 months later

All figures, interest rate used and time frame are just for demonstration purposes and the word 'anticipated' is not implied as a prediction of a specific moment in time

* This is the approximate amount of money to have aside in redraw or funds acccessible to cover the interest repayments on the debt until a prospective tenant can be found.

Figure 6 is a typical breakdown of the progress payments to build a house on land owned or recently purchased. It is worth borrowing enough to cover the interest repayment cost of the increasing debt up until the property is built and ready to either move into or rent out. Obviously, there will be no rent coming in from the property during construction, but the debt is increasing as the dwelling progresses towards completion.

Completion may be approximately six to eight months after titles are registered, and land purchased. The names of the five progress payments or stages are: slab, frame, lock up, fit out, and practical completion (then the certificate of occupancy is issued). The percentages are standard in both examples and are based on an HIA (Housing Industry Association) compliant contract. Occasionally, lenders will agree to percentages that are not in line with HIA standards.

LMI: Should You Have It or Should You Avoid It?

Another consideration is whether you should take out Lenders Mortgage Insurance (LMI). If used correctly, LMI can be a borrower's best friend, since it allows investors to get into the property market or apply for a loan increase without requiring the cash that they otherwise would have needed. Buying a home/investment property is often a balancing act between borrowing more to preserve cash and borrowing less to preserve debt-servicing capacity, extra LMI cost, and cost of the debt. LMI is for the protection of lenders (paid by the client) in the event that they default on the loan. It is a once-off premium that can often be added to the loan. It is not a mortgage protection fee for the client.

Using or avoiding LMI can be, in part, determined by the amount of equity a person has available and/or how much of their cash or equity they want to use or preserve for the next purchase. It can be both a useful tool or a millstone depending on how it is employed, and depending on the underlying asset. And while rules of thumb are helpful, there are always considerations and exceptions.

It is important to remember that the more you borrow, the higher the repayments, which in turn will eat into your cash flow. If LMI is added to the loan, you will also pay interest on this additional debt, over and above interest on your loan. LMI forms part of the cost base of the property as well, meaning that the property will need to increase in value to compensate for the LMI cost if it is added to the loan. The cost base refers to the price you paid for it, and any costs associated with the qcuisition of the property (in general terms).

LMI can be costly, and the price becomes higher as the loan amount and LVR increase. For example, the LMI charge on a $700,000 investment property purchase at an LVR of 90% may be approximately $17,000. In comparison, for a $650,000 purchase at 85% LVR, the LMI may be approximately $6,800.

LMI is usually not portable. If a borrower refinances their loan to another lender to seek a cheaper rate, they will pay the LMI all over again if they exceed the 80% LVR (based on a full documentation loan). The premium paid the first time around is, for the most part, gone.

The cost of stamp duty may have a bearing on the need to use LMI, since a person's cash or equity may only be enough to complete the purchase, but not enough for stamp duty as well. This could lead to them needing to borrow more against the property.

I have written a large section in Property Finance Made Simple on how to improve your chances of borrowing money initially and then borrowing more. I recommend reading it in full, but I have included a summary here.

Given every lender is different in how they assess your income and your liabilities, it is important to get the choice of lender correct to begin with.

If someone wishes to continue to purchase investment property, it is important to use different lenders to suit their purpose and the type of loan required. They also need to consider the type of property they are purchasing, the strength of their income in servicing the loan, and their existing exposure to the lender.

The first step in considering applying for a loan, and improving the chances of success each time, is understanding the household living expenses and having a budget. There are a number of things a borrower can do to improve their own ability to borrow more money.

A very useful budgeting calculator (for your living expenses) can be found at ASIC's MoneySmart website (www.moneysmart.gov.au). Be honest with yourself when using it. You will be provided a reasonably good indication of what may be possible. Become more accountable to yourself. This can provide a well-needed boost to a deposit for a property.

Investing in property requires planning and it involves having several strategies. Success in growing a property portfolio is not only about the property values increasing, it is also about balancing your accessible equity/cash available with your ability to service debt.

Consider reducing any credit card limit; your borrowing capacity will increase immediately. Most lenders factor in 3% per month for a credit card limit; not on what is owing, but, rather, the full limit. For every $1000 that you remove from your credit card limit, you can increase your borrowing capacity by up to $5500, depending on the lender.

Be prepared and organised; keep your paperwork up to date.

Age of Property

Consider whether you are buying a new versus established property and the state in which you plan to buy. The stamp duty differences between states are huge, such as the stamp duty paid for established rather than new property (again, avoid off-the-plan).

Repayment Type and Frequency

When there is a loan you would like to reduce, consider weekly or fortnightly repayments. Interest is compounded daily — you pay interest on interest, so every day that goes by is another day interest is added (after being calculated on the debt, plus all the days of interest charged prior, between the last repayment to the next).

Offset and Access

Instead of putting money into the loan, an offset account could store the money whilst saving/offsetting interest on the loan.

Avoid family pledge (using your property or income to help someone else get a loan), and avoid being a guarantor or co-borrower with anyone other than perhaps your defacto partner or partner through marriage, even then, pleasue ensure you are very happy together

Ownership Structure

Establishing the correct foundation through structuring is vital. Capital gains must be apportioned according to the ownership on the title, not according to who is on the loan. A borrower on the mortgage has no entitlement of ownership, profit, or rent associated with the property if they are not on the title.

Strategies for Buying Multiple Investment Properties

I am going to focus here on the financing strategies that should be considered to help make multiple property purchases.

Criteria to Borrow Money

When it comes to obtaining finance to purchase property, there are three main criteria to meet in order to more likely get the green light.

1. *Maintain a good credit rating (or at least not a bad one). Make sure you are always on top of your financial commitments and pay your bills on time so that you hopefully never end up with any black marks on your credit file.*

2. *Have enough cash/equity for the deposit to cover the gap between what the bank will lend you and the total cost to acquire the property.*

3. *Show that you have enough income to service the debt you already have and that you are asking for. This will be through the income you receive from your job/company, Centrelink, and the rent from your property or properties.*

If you can tick all three boxes, then there is more reason for the banks to consider your loan application favourably.

Principal & Interest Versus Interest-only Loans

Interest-only (I/O)

For a period of time, usually five to ten years, the borrower only has to make interest repayments on the mortgage, and does not need to pay back any of the money borrowed during this period. Many, if not most, investors do this for all of their investment properties to aid them in building a portfolio. It can assist first-home buyers with cash flow on their home, since it reduces their repayment commitment, helping them deal with the cost of furniture and moving. A one year interest-only period may be suitable for some people to help with managing the cost of the loan. It provides more surplus for 'would be' investors, therefore making it easier to afford holding a negatively geared property. It can assist in providing greater serviceability on a lender's calculator. Pre-2016, lenders used to assess interest-only repayments in their serviceability calculators at actual repayments, but this has changed for almost all lenders. Most now assess all existing debt as they do new debt, at a qualifying rate of above 7%, usually 7.2–7.4%. Genworth Financial, one of the largest mortgage insurers in the market, has been using a qualifying rate of 8%, even though the repayments may be below 5% on the new loan and existing loans. A couple of lenders still assess existing debts at actual repayments rather than a higher qualifying repayment rate. Therefore, interest only (I/O) loans can be very useful in calculating someone's borrowing capacity on serviceability calculators with these lenders, mitigating the reduction of borrowing capacity associated with the servicing of a debt.

In relation to a bank's servicing calculator, your borrowing capacity will be reduced or increased depending on the lender chosen if you elect for an interest only period. The particular lender could factor in that you will have to repay the entire loan in only twenty-five years rather than thirty years (based on the first five years of the 30-year loan term being an interest-only period, meaning the period over which principal is paid is only twenty-five years long). This places pressure on servicing. It is a balancing act in playing around with these variations to provide the most suitable outcome for an individual borrower.

Wisely chosen lenders can often assist in overcoming some of the above issues or, as some say, impediments. Borrowers risk being caught off guard if they have too many loans set up as interest-only. When the loan(s) does convert to principal and interest (P&I), the repayments will jump up considerably for two reasons.

1. *Previously the borrower was only making interest-only repayments on the debt; now they are paying back the debt in increments as well as still paying interest.*
2. *The increments of debt now being paid back are condensed into the remaining life of the loan, say twenty to twenty-five years (the remaining life of the original 30-year loan, based on a five- to ten-year period of interest-only). This makes the increment of debt each week, fortnight, or month much higher than if a P&I loan was taken out to begin with, and spread over the 30-year life of the loan.*

Many investors, to avoid this higher, more condensed repayment schedule, used to refinance to another lender on a standard 30-year term (sometimes a 40-year loan term). This has become more difficult.

After ASIC carried out a cost comparison, it was found that a borrower could pay $32,000 more in interest repayments over the life of the loan if they elected for a five-year interest-only loan compared to a P&I loan, and over $80,000 more in interest repayments if the interest-only period was ten years long.

Many will argue that it is okay to not reduce investment debt because it allows you to borrow a larger amount for more properties and therefore create greater wealth. Until recently, it has been relatively straightforward for a borrower to refinance a loan every five years in order to continue for yet another five-year loan term at I/O. Property marketing companies (spruikers) may float wonderful-sounding capital growth figures, with relatively low cost of holding the asset, by keeping your loans interest-only.

I caution you to be careful – it is becoming more difficult to find lenders where all boxes can be ticked, and if you keep accumulating debt without reducing it, your position becomes more precarious. Most importantly, pay off the home loan and consider not having an interest-only loan on it. By all means, consider having interest-only on an investment loan when a home loan debt is in place. But once the home loan debt is paid off, consider reducing the investment debt. Many lenders now offer better rates to borrowers who ask for P&I loans on investment debt anyway.

Principal and Interest (P&I)

These loans have higher repayments than interest-only loans, as some of the repayment is going towards reducing the loan principal (debt amount) over the life of the loan. If the borrower has a home loan, and that loan was not for the purpose of investment, then no tax benefits are in play, so many borrowers prefer to concentrate on paying down their home loan before reducing a debt they may have for an investment property.

In the early years of the term of the loan, the majority of the repayment is interest, while only a small amount is principal. It is often considered better to have fortnightly repayments, rather than monthly, due to the fact that lenders compound the interest every day — in other words, they charge interest not only on the loan amount, but also on the interest charged on the loan amount each day until the repayment comes out. If you pay fortnightly, the compounding interest is less costly. The more frequently a repayment is made and any accrued interest is paid and cleared, the cost of the compounding effect on the borrower is lower. This will be covered in more detail later in the book.

Over time, the principal component of the repayment starts to form a great part of the regular payment on the loan. One of the main reasons that the first years of repayments consist mainly of interest is because the lender is *not* a not-for-profit organisation. They are a business, and they only care about their shareholders and profit margin. Banks are not in the business of lending money. They are in the business of making money by lending it to you and, given the average time a person remains with their lender is 3.5 years, it makes sense that lenders want to make as much money as possible during that time.

Every time you refinance, you start the 30-year loan term all over again, effectively going backwards, and costing you much more interest over the life of the loan.

Figure 7 shows how with an interest only loan over 30 years, none of the original loan is reduced, you would still have this debt. This is scary! Of course, there are no 30 year interest only loans available, but a borrower could, in theory, continue to refinance their interest only loan indefinitely. In this example, the loan type is a variable rate, not a fixed rate loan. The cost of the loan, without reducing any of the debt, would be $668,250 just in interest.

Whilst the interest repayments slope downward, this is purely demonstrating the finite term of the loan, so at the end of 30 years, the term would end and the principle amount of $500,000 would have to be repaid in full.

In Figure 8: a principle and interest loan is represented, the total interest cost over the life of the loan would be $407,913. The borrower would save over $260,000. Imagine the savings on several properties, having principle and interest rather than interest only loans.

Figure 7

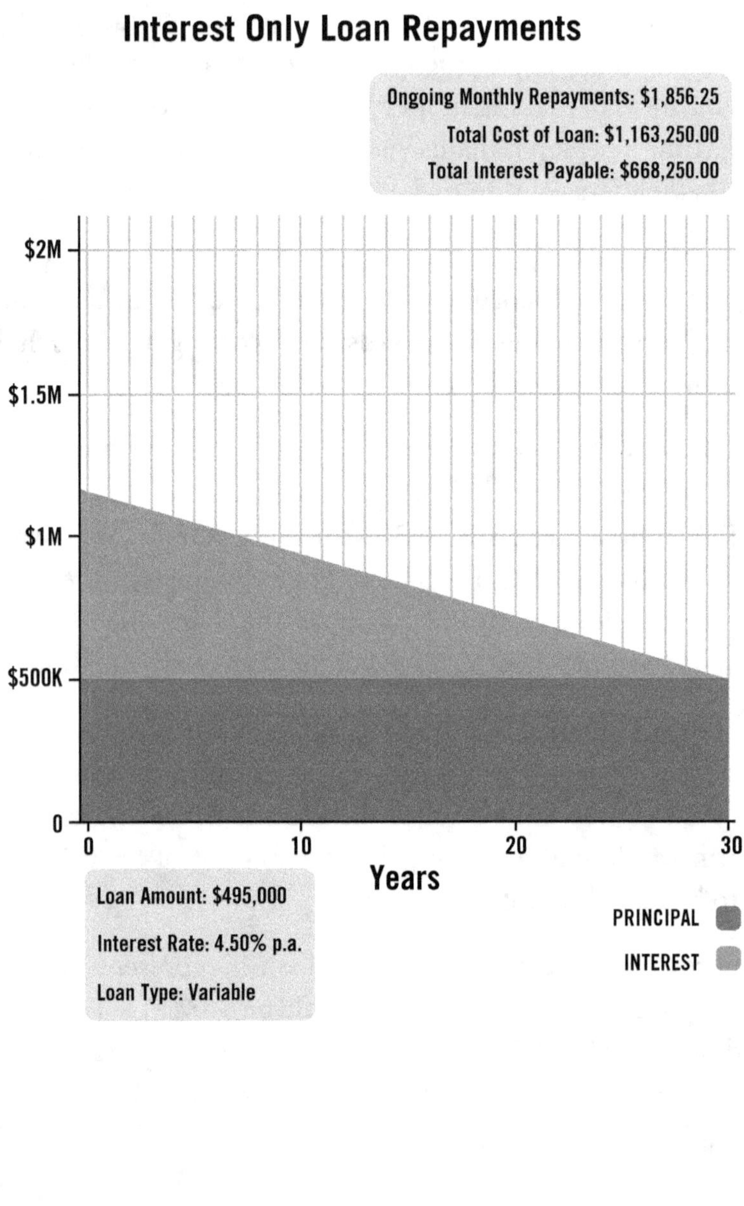
Interest Only Loan Repayments
Ongoing Monthly Repayments: $1,856.25
Total Cost of Loan: $1,163,250.00
Total Interest Payable: $668,250.00
$2M
$1.5M
$1M
$500K
0
0
10
20
30
Years
Loan Amount: $495,000
Interest Rate: 4.50% p.a.
Loan Type: Variable
PRINCIPAL
INTEREST

Figure 8

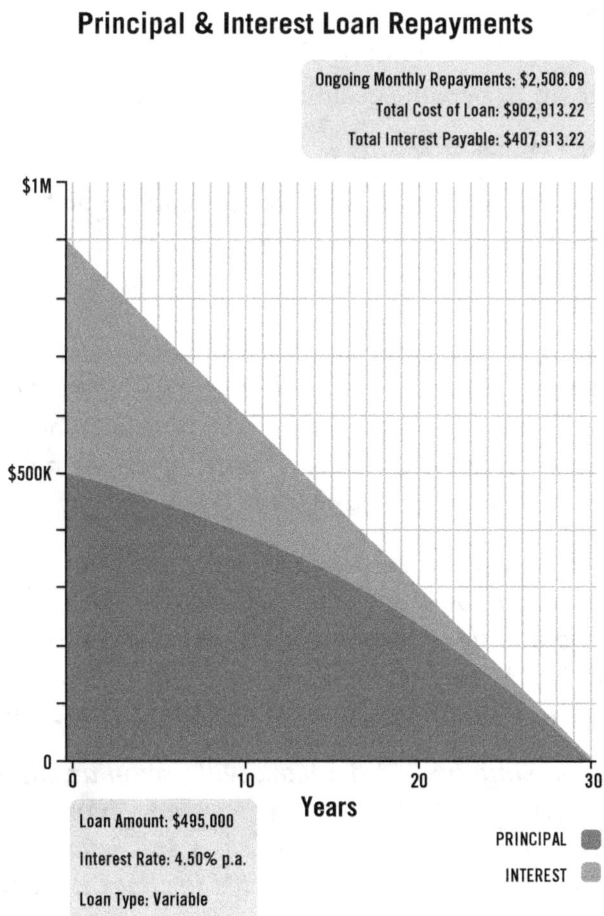

Note: Always have a SMART goal. It must be specific, measurable, attainable, relevant to you, and focused on a fixed point in time. To fill in an Investment Readiness Questionnaire, please go to australianpropertyadvisorygroup/resources

Putting Together Your Lending Structure and Strategy

Now, I want to run through an approach that has been used by several people to maximise their financing opportunities. The scenario below is based on an actual lender's policy in each instance.

Scenario

Sam and Jane want to set up their core banking with a lender who will assist them to become established and therefore ready for their investment journey.

Bank A assesses Sam and Jane's borrowing capacity at a rate of 7.25%. Bank A has the following policies when assessing borrowing capacity.

- *Bank A allows deductible interest add backs (i.e. interest expense) borrowing no more than 90% of the property's value (note: the maximum loan to value ratio for an investment with this lender is 90%, hence the reference to borrowing no more than 90%).*
- *Bank A assesses existing mortgage debts at the actual interest rate on a principal and interest basis, based on the remaining term of the loan, and then Bank A adds a 20% buffer. This applies to the mortgages already with the bank, as well as the new mortgage being applied for.*
- *The maximum yield the bank will use on an investment property is 6%. Some properties are more positively geared than this, so in some cases this lender could be a disadvantage. However, in this instance it works well, when in conjunction with the rest of the strategy.*

These criteria are not the most generous assessment criteria in the market, but it is a good place to start for these clients as it suits them strategically (i.e. to maximise an overall borrowing plan). This becomes clearer as we move to the next bank.

When the borrowing capacity is exhausted with Bank A, it is time to use Bank B.

Bank B assesses existing debts which the clients have with other lenders at the actual repayment, and then add a buffer of 30% to that payment amount. This is a more generous assessment than Bank A if the existing loan is interest-only, because Bank B applies the buffer to the interest-only repayments, unlike Bank A, where the repayments are converted to principal and interest for the buffer to be applied to.

Let's look at some figures to see what this difference in assessment criteria looks like between the two banks. Based on a $450,000 interest-only loan for the first five years at an interest rate of 4.5%, the monthly repayment would be $1,687.5.

Bank A would assess this scenario as follows: $450,000 principal and interest repayments over twenty-five years equates to $2741.94 per month, and a 20% buffer will be added to that on the borrowing capacity calculator. This means that the payment amount they would assume for testing borrowing capacity would be $3,290 per month.

Bank B would assess as follows: take the $1,687.5 per month, and add a 30% buffer. For testing borrowing capacity, the figure becomes $2,193.75 per month, a difference of $1,096.25 per month lower than Bank A. This creates a significant positive increase in Sam and Jane's borrowing capacity.

The second key reason why Bank B is the better option at this stage, only after previously using Bank A, is because Bank B adds a buffer rate of 7.4% to all debt, after first converting any interest-only loans to principal and interest. Using Bank B before Bank A would disadvantage the borrower if they already had multiple loans with Bank B. It is an advantage to a Sam and Jane if they use Bank B after Bank A, as they have mortgages with other lenders, and those mortgages remain where they are.

Both Banks A and B allow for deductible interest in the borrowing capacity calculator and apply a maximum of 6% yield.

Once the client has exhausted their borrowing capacity with Banks A and B, their broker turned to Bank C for the additional lending required for the next property.

There are a number of key factors, which make Bank C the lender of choice for this next phase. These factors are:*Bank C assess existing debts at the actual repayments with no buffer loading.*

- *There is no maximum rental yield that can be used for assessment.*
- *They allow deductible interest add backs, just like Bank A and B.*
- *The assessment rate they use for new money borrowed is one of the lowest in the marketplace, with an interest rate margin added to the actual repayment interest rate (rather than applying a larger buffer rate of 7.4%, for example).*

All of these factors maximise Sam and Jane's borrowing capacity.

There have been many scenarios I have come across where investors feel they have hit a brick wall when it comes to obtaining more finance to expand their portfolio. I have just explained how to achieve maximum capacity based on a borrower's individual circumstances. This could not have been achieved as seamlessly without a broker — the borrower would not have known which lenders to choose at each appropriate time, and each lender would have myopically offered their own products. This highlights how critical it is to not only understand how lenders may assess your borrowing capacity, but also how important it is to think strategically. Who has the time or knowledge to do this themselves?

I would like to finish this section by saying that regardless of what a lender, or suite of lenders, will allow you to borrow, and regardless of whether you are buying a principal place of residence or an investment property, it is critically important as a buyer that you are comfortable with the level of debt you take on. You must have a comprehensive plan that considers a whole range of factors, so that you can make your own assessment on the suitability of each credit transaction you enter into. This should not be limited to your property purchasing plan, but it should also take into consideration other factors in your life.

Debt you access needs to be manageable and sustainable in the short term, but more importantly over the long term. That way, if rates rise, which they will, and any interest-only loans convert to principal and interest, this means that you can cope and are not forced to offload any property. With a thorough plan, you will enjoy the benefits that come with buying real estate and you will be well-prepared to deal with whatever comes your way.

CHAPTER 4

Research (Reduce Risk, Improve Potential)

Once you have a plan in place and it has been decided what you should/need to buy, what your budget is, and the required number of properties, then you start the research. There are many strategies that should and will be considered in a good plan and a combination is required to put together an effective tailored plan. Firstly, let's look at what research is.

What is Research and Due Diligence?

Everyone seems to have an answer to this question. Many investors are drawn towards innuendo, media hype, and listening to friends, family, and backyard experts. Everybody has an opinion. The real issue, which inadvertently leads to failure, lies in not undertaking proper research. Some people kid themselves into believing that merely reading a glossy brochure about some house and land package or off-the-plan project is sufficient, and that the salesperson is believable and trustworthy. I strongly beg to differ!

There is no real rulebook out there, until now…

Here are some respectable and risk-reducing considerations that should make your job easier in finding an outperforming location. This also reinforces why it is important to seek objective advice. I will provide an overview in this next section.

Components of Research

Let's start with the reality of any property. There is no guarantee. There is no magic wand. Some people sell answers to what they call 'secrets.' There are no secrets. However, if you do not do your research, you are planning to fail. By researching, you are reducing your risk by eliminating some very obvious negatives that could be associated with an area. This serves to reduce your chances of failing, and therefore increase your chances of success.

"If anyone presents themselves as a holder of 'secrets' in real estate, run away. Don't look back. Anyone promising to reveal secrets in the property business is, by definition, a spruiker." — **Terry Ryder**

Looking at supply and demand, many marketing firms and spruikers (who have vested interests and incentives attached to specific locations and projects) will tell you how good the population migration is and, maybe, what the Government is planning to spend in the area. They excite you with the fittings and fixtures included in the project, and this can lead to many investors immediately forgetting that every other apartment in the development has the same or similar inclusions. The major hole in their story is what the supply and demand is in the area. They tend to ignore this fundamental part of research, and conveniently misrepresent population migration, as it is not taken into context with supply and demand. The fundamental figures start with supply and demand, like any commodity. If there is no demand, then it has little true value.

The location of the suburb is a good starting point. Its proximity to desired services and infrastructure (e.g. transport, jobs, schools, entertainment, medical) is the driving force attracting people to the area. If people are not attracted to the area, why would the area increase in value? Some places have the benefits of a sea change; some have the benefits of the country. The more important elements of the location are its infrastructure. Some infrastructure is merely 'being discussed' with the council and other authorities as to whether it will be planned. Then it may end up 'being planned,' and move forward to being a 'committed plan.' Once the infrastructure has actually commenced, you can be more certain that it is in full swing and it will have a tangible end result. The best solution here is to select a location where there are several existing industries. Be careful if you are acting on something that is only being discussed. It needs to be approved.

Mining towns, for example, may only have mining as an industry. You can lose a great deal — not just in capital growth potential, but through real growth decline. Rental property often declines significantly in a one-industry town. If the industry falters, the town could die. You need a location where people will stay regardless. The economy of the area and surrounds, including the amenities already there (and in the pipeline), is important to know. Properties in suburbs with train stations tend to grow more than suburbs without stations in metropolitan locations. Hospitals, schools, other transport, and shops are important too.

The demographics of the location are significant, particularly for guiding you in making a more informed decision about the 'what' you should buy in the area. Demographics are very important for your budget, growth, rental, any works needed on the property, and whether those renovations will improve the value. They also tell you the number of renters in the area. It is very handy if you can find out how many investors are buying in the same development you are looking at, and over what timeframe the dwellings are being released. In some areas, units are more popular and will have appeal to a greater percentage of the population. In other areas, duplexes or houses are better.

Vacancy rates (not just the current rates, but also how they are trending) will help you see if the area is becoming more popular, or losing residents. A simple snapshot will not demonstrate this, as it only captures a moment in time. When you look at investing in shares, you would normally look at trends, so why not do the same with property?

The methodology applies to the following market indicators:

- *Capital growth history*
- *Yields*
- *Actual rental income (in dollars rather than yield)*
- *Median house prices*
- *Local Economy*
- *Days on Market*
- *Government spending*
- *Supply and demand*
    - Tenant demand
    - Supply of stock
    - Industries
    - Population
    - Job security
    - Education
    - Land
    - Amenities
    - Stock on market
    - Number of sales
    - Auction clearance rates
    - Vendor discounts
    - Discounting

- *Demographic*
- *Wage trend*
- *Affordability*
- *Ripple effect*
- *Comparable Sales*
- *Proximity to train stations and other amenities (Walk Score, Google Earth)*
- *Appeal and suitability of the property and its inclusions*
- *Gentrification*

Narrow down the location, based on borrowing capacity and strategy. Bear in mind the basics of supply versus demand in conjunction with population growth, and infrastructure that is supporting employment and employment growth. It must be a multi-industry suburb to avoid excessive risk. Check whether the infrastructure growth is temporary. Will people (e.g. tradespeople, construction workers) leave once everything is built? Will vacancy rates increase after construction is completed (particularly if developers move in like moths to a flame and overdevelop an area)? Check the position that the state is in, regarding the property cycle.

The property cycle is the period of time over which the price of a property increases or declines by being influenced from demographic, economic, and supply and demand changes in the area, or nearby areas which could have a ripple effect. Each area may have its own cycle and be at different stages than others — at the bottom, middle, or top of the cycle. It is always a good time to buy somewhere, but *not* everywhere at any given time.

Oversupply, master-planned communities, and excess land can all hinder growth. Prime examples could be suburbs in growth corridors, as there could be better opportunities further in towards the CBD, or even in locations the same distance from the CBD. In some of these large estates, schools, hospitals, shopping centres, and a train station are all aiding the benefits of your potential property. Trains and access to transport are big factors in the investment being viable.

If you follow this process, you can dramatically enhance your ability to time the market, take more advantage of outperforming potential, reduce risk, and balance the effect on your lifestyle — and better your future!

Budget, affordability, your attitude, your tailored plan, and the research undertaken will influence the following choices.

- *The state within Australia that you should purchase the next property in. This could change for each property.*
- *Metro or regional location.*

If it is a metro location, then further refinement will be required:

- *Metro 1: within 10km of the CBD*
- *Metro 2: within 20km of the CBD*
- *Metro 3: within 30km of the CBD*
- *Fringe: 30km–40km from the CBD*
- *Metro: satellite cities/growing hubs*

If regional locations suit you, then investigate which regional hubs are the best.

Research must be based on facts and figures, and reliable, unbiased information. This goes for information provided to the investor, and the information the investor is basing their own decision on as well. Often property investors can fall into the trap of using their own emotions, beliefs, attitudes, and experiences to base decisions on, such as where to buy, what to buy, and the inclusions in the property itself.

What you or I may personally prefer has no relevance when compared to what the area suggests is needed, in reference to the type of dwelling, what is more suitable to the demographic, and the type of dwelling that will appeal to more people.

Locations are in cycles, peaks, and troughs, periods of growth and decline. Check the position on the property cycle clock that the desired location is in. On a clock, the peak would be 12 o'clock (at the end of the boom) and 6 o'clock would be the trough (the bottom of the market). Between 12 o'clock and 3 o'clock is a correction. During the 3 o'clock to 5 o'clock period, buying in the area must be avoided. 5 o'clock to 9 o'clock provides opportunity. It is difficult to know when the top or bottom is going to be. At 10 o'clock and 11 o'clock, you might want to exercise caution, and 12 o'clock means stop.

There is no perfect answer to this. An investor would be interested in understanding the trend in growth, the percentage of growth per annum, the consistency in growth, and the average growth each year (and over three years, five years, and ten years). The problem is that a decision to invest cannot only rely on whether the suburb has increased continually, rapidly, or by a huge amount in isolation to any other data. Some people believe in investing in an area that has seen these traits, but what if the property has gone through its growth cycle, is at its peak, and may be heading towards a stabilisation period or is starting to trend slightly down? Or, it could be at 9'oclock in its property cycle, and may be worth considering then.

The market needs to be understood. An opportunity may arise whereby the suburb has not seen much growth, but rents have been rising, which could mean considering whether growth may then start to increase. Likewise, it could have gone through the downward cycle or be at the bottom of the property clock, in which case it may be time to consider buying in that area.

Example of a Property Clock

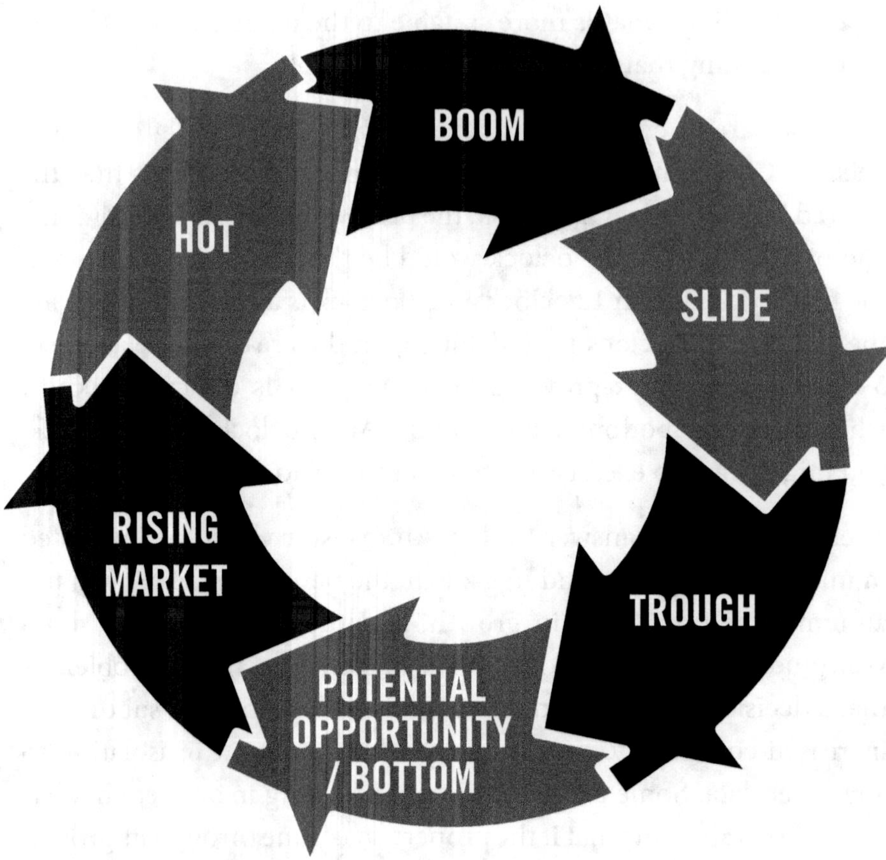

Peak/Boom – 12 o'clock

Avoid buying at this time; whether you are buying the property to live in or for investment, you will pay too much. This is a seller's market, not a buyer's market: difficult to negotiate, and discounts are small.

Downturn/Slide – 12 o'clock to 3 o'clock

Prices and rents tend to start declining; the herd is still in denial, thinking prices will keep rising.

Gloom/Trough – 3 o'clock to 6 o'clock

Prices will start obviously dropping. This can be a longer phase, with the bottom not necessarily in sight. Confidence has dropped significantly, auction clearance rates are down, and days on market are longer. Yields are either dropping further or remaining steady.

Bottom and Opportunity – 6 o'clock

This is a buyer's market. Discounts are high, easy to negotiate, and sellers are more desperate. Buyers can take their time.

Recovery to Rising market – 6 o'clock to 10 o'clock

The safest time to buy is probably between 7:30 to 9:30 for many investors. It is more obvious at this point that the market has bottomed.

Hot/Approaching Peak – 10 o'clock to 12 o'clock

The market is in a frenzy and gets too hot to buy. Around 10 o'clock the market still has some last-minute opportunities and a small window remains, but it is riskier. Demand is very high.

The location could also be going through a gentrification transition, and it is time to consider buying. Most people just follow the herd. More successful investors get in earlier, but, of course, getting in too early is riskier and more speculative. It is a gamble of risk for return, in some ways. At least property has less volatility than shares, for example.

Consumer Sentiment

Consumer sentiment measures the confidence level people have about the economy, and about their job security and income stability. The less confidence people have, the less they spend. This has a direct correlation to GDP (Gross Domestic Product). GDP is the measure of the value of the goods and services produced by a country in a given period of time. The lower GDP is, the worse the country's economic position is. A reduction in GDP often leads to fewer jobs, and economic instability. A reduction in GDP can be due to rising interest rates, or people spending less due to perceived job insecurity. Inflation can also lead to people spending less as things become less affordable, which in turn leads to a lower GDP. Consumer confidence around current market conditions and their expectations for the future is an important factor for the state of the economy.

It is something that investors should understand and consider, but no matter how low sentiment may be, there will always be property investment purchase opportunities worth pursuing. Of course, if sentiment is low, auction clearance rates often decline and prices may stabilise (in some places, they will drop) as demand for property and consumer spending drops. Vendor discounting will rise in an effort to sell their property. At higher price levels, prices will probably decline more. At lower price levels, prices could decline less, or remain more stable, partly because more people can afford lower prices than higher prices and also because the areas may not have seen the massive artificial growth that some more expensive places have seen.

Looking at supply and demand, in conjunction with population migration, is one of the most important points. There are several places with oversupply issues and extremely high vacancy rates. Some high density, inner city suburbs may be nice to live in, but they do not necessarily make for a smart investment.

If, however, you look at population migration in isolation, you may be led to believe an area like Docklands, Victoria is a perfect area to invest, because it is very close to Melbourne CBD, and quick and easy to commute to work in the CBD from. Normally, proximity to amenities, jobs, and transport leads to capital growth, but if you have oversupply, like in Docklands, you will forever be competing against other investors to rent your property out or to sell it. It will more likely earn less and lose money. Hence why it is so important to review population growth with the supply of property in the area. If people are not attracted to the area, the area is unlikely to increase in value.

Some people wait until the value of the location is slapping them in the face before it dawns on them that it may be worth buying there. By then, it is often too late. The best solution is to select a location where there are several existing industries. You must avoid one-industry towns, because if government contracts cease or spending dries up, and the population is very small, the town will probably die. Capital values will drop and vacancy rates will rocket up, while rental income and yields will plummet down.

Demographic data also tells you the number of renters in an area. If an area is predominately renters and not home owners, it risks becoming a slum. The number of renters versus owners will impact on the upkeep and future desirability of pockets within a suburb. Tenants often have little to no regard for the garden and general upkeep. There will always be competition with other landlords when trying to sell or rent out the property, leading to less profit and/or less rental income.

Many people think that when a property has been on the market for two months, nobody wants it. I see opportunity. Maybe the vendor has been out of touch with reality of what the property is really worth. The agent normally has signed a three-month contract to sell it, which means that both the vendor and agent may be more pliable and agreeable to a lower price. Look at the best streets; try to stay within a couple of blocks of these.

Comparable sales and timing of these is very handy and vital to your negotiations. You can compare what similar properties sold for within the previous six months, preferably within three months (this is what valuers and financial institutions use). Use this as ammunition; it provides you confidence in what the property may be worth. It is best to look out for sales within 1km (others which are a little further away in the same suburb may still be okay). Compare land size within 10% or less variance, or for buildings, compare the same number of bedrooms and bathrooms. There is software that will do all of this for you, or, preferably, you can use a buyer's agent.

If the property is new or not yet built, focus on fittings and fixtures included in the property, their quality, and their uniqueness. But be aware of what other properties in the estate include.

There are ways which allow you to drill down in a suburb and overlay your own preferences to find an ideal location. Figures suggest choosing the street wisely can deliver much more capital growth, rather than haphazardly buying in a suburb. You may wish to understand which streets have less public housing and streets where residents earn more than in other streets. Rent and yield is higher in some parts of a suburb and you can avoid pockets of a suburb with too many units or apartments, or with too high a percentage of tenants versus owner-occupiers.

A good buyer's agent will have access to several analysis tools that, on aggregate, would cost a significant amount per year to subscribe to. Leveraging off a buyer's agent and their access to data and knowledge can save you thousands in annual subscriptions for the same outcome, not to mention hundreds of thousands in buying the right property. Doing it on your own is fraught with danger, without leveraging off the experience and knowledge of someone more qualified.

You can consider non-quantifiable facts, such as a future planned infrastructure like a new shopping centre, school, or train station, accessibility to schools, childcare, medical centres, arterial links, perceived gentrification, Walk Score, council plans, or other property developments. Whilst some of these will have a very explicit impact on the area, you cannot definitely compare intangible information with one suburb to another. They are intangible if they are at the planning or consideration stage. Once they are approved, confirmed, and given the green light, then they become tangible. These core drivers of attraction to the suburb will be creating demand and they need to be considered in correlation with hard figures, tangible information, statistics, and trend analysis. The problem is that there is a level of subjectivity applied to intangibles and unquantifiable information, and actual figures are important to narrow down the margin of error.

When analysing intangible data with tangible data, you can track the change in a trend to see when there is an impact from the intangible things happening in the suburb. Consider, also, that the actual property must have appeal to another owner-occupier and resident of the area. So, street appeal, crime rates, and noise pollution are also factors that may contradict what may be promising on the surface. We need to rely heavily on a *combination* of data, so we must try to determine the level of reliability of each set of data being used.

Comparing data of different measurable factors allows you to weed out anomalies and inconsistencies. It is always wise to consider the data showing trends over a sufficient period of time; if it is too short a time, it is less reliable. If you look at data that is too little, then what you look at is less reliable. Ensure the data is sound. Look for whether it is a paid promotion, or if it is core data from, for example, the Australian Bureau of Statistics. You cannot compare tangible figures that are too similar either, so you need to consider variables/points that create differences between suburbs.

Watch out for the trend in data. Do not buy at the start of a trend you think will happen; jump in when it is obvious there is a trend, but before it has been trending for too long. How long is too long is the same as the saying, "how long is a piece of string?" If you wait a couple of years, or wait until you see it on TV or see it being reinforced by many others, you have probably left it too late.

Once you have decided upon which state you should buy in, the local government area (LGA) of your desired suburb(s) would be considered. LGAs include several suburbs under one council and may all be benefiting from infrastructure or incompetence from council. It is handy to compare a suburb within the LGA to the LGA itself. Transport, population growth, and general appeal can vary across the suburbs, as can the level of income people are earning, dwelling type, and socio-demographic.

Someone once told me if you look after the big rocks, the small rocks will look after themselves. Property is similar in some ways. If you focus on the macro research and systematically drill down to a choice of suburbs, taking your situation and strategy into account, you can then focus on the micro elements of due diligence. There is no point assessing a suburb until you have determined that the suburb is the best choice for your plan. It is 80% about location, and 20% about the specific property within this location.

Statistics and data are so important in order to avoid emotional, ad hoc, and ill-informed decisions. You should avoid subjectivity.

Capital Growth

Whilst historical performance may or may not be a possible indicator of future performance, past performance can be considered as a reasonable starting point to compare the growth (over the last five years, for example) in one suburb to another. If the suburb has seen excellent growth, there must be reasons why. The more those reasons are understood, the more a determination can be made as to whether the growth has reached its peak or if it may continue. Suburbs nearby may be worth investigating. They may not have seen the same growth, but could benefit from the ripple effect. It is arguably less risky to buy somewhere that has seen good growth due to confirmed reasons (rather than an anomaly) than to buy in an area that has had little to no growth. Of course, there may be factors that could soon lead to great growth in a suburb that has not seen much lately. Hence the importance of further research.

Advertised Median Rent

With advertised median rent, it is good to understand the actual dollars involved. The drivers in an area that will influence growth and yield (demand and supply) are not measurable; they are more subjective as to their influence.

Gross Rental Yield

Gross Rental Yield is based on the rent per week, multiplied by the fifty-two weeks of the year. Divide the figure into the median property price, then multiply by 100, which gives you a percentage. This excludes property holding costs, but is very handy to gauge the annual return for that suburb and property over another. For positive cash flow, you may need to look for over 6.5%, depending on interest rates and other property costs.

Talk to rental managers about what tenants prefer, such as pockets within the suburb, favoured streets, inclusions, or any upgrades that could improve the rent. Compare yield increases and rent dollar increases. Yield would be trending down as growth trends up in a good growth area. Is the tenant demand all year or seasonal? Coincide the tenancy agreement with the season.

For example, some regional locations have universities and they have an influx of students at the end of the year. Therefore, contrary to standard locations, locations that have a large university population would lead to getting a tenancy contract signed in December. Everywhere else, this is often the worst time to sign contracts as most people are thinking about Christmas, not the instability and hassle of moving.

Number Sold

The total sales figures provide an insight into the local market. Higher seller activity could represent higher demand; it is wise to look at the related trends. Sales growth is often followed by price increases, whereas sales declines are followed by price declines.

Auction Clearance Rates

Auction clearance rates are a sign of demand. Above 60% indicates a healthy, balanced market, and above 80% indicates high demand. However, this is not necessarily data that applies to every suburb. In blue chip and more salubrious suburbs, it is more the norm to auction a property. The same rules apply to auction clearance rates as they do to other indicators. The suburb could be near its peak, and you could end up paying a very high price, so get in early when the trend has an upward trajectory, rather than waiting until it has become a seller's market. If the clearance rate is low, this could indicate that demand is down, and not at the level where it would need to be to consider buying in that suburb. Again, a trend is necessary to form a picture, rather than just looking at a moment in time.

Days on Market

The average number of days a property is on the market around the country is approximately 85–95 days. If a property is sold quicker than this, it indicates higher demand. But much longer than this, and it may be best to look in a different area. If there is less demand, too much supply, or it is any area not worth buying in, the longer time it will take to sell the property. The more days that pass while it is on the market, the more it becomes a buyer's market. Many people tend to believe that the longer a property has been on the market, the greater likelihood there is that something is wrong with it. Providing all other research stacks up, a property that has been sitting on the market for a lengthy period of time could be an opportunity to buy at a good price.

If the days on market are shorter (a reasonable guideline could be under 90 days), then that indicates it is more of a seller's market, due to buyer demand. This means that sellers have more of an upper hand, and vendor discounting would typically be lower. In other words, vendors would not have to drop their price or negotiate as much, and the buyer would have less leverage in negotiating.

Vacancy Rates (Demand)

The national average for vacancy rates is typically 3%, so it is important to consider buying in a suburb with vacancy rates beneath this figure. Look for a lower percentage, as this would represent higher demand. A higher figure could represent low demand or oversupply. Also consider that a slightly higher vacancy rate in a suburb with both older and newer houses could mean that renters want a newer place to live rather than the older stock available. This may seem to support buying a new property, but it does not necessarily represent a good capital growth opportunity to buy new instead of established. If the vacancy rate is really low, around 1% or lower, it could mean there is upward pressure on rents and yields could then increase.

Stock on Market (Supply)

A correlation should be made between the number of properties sold and the trend of this data. If this trend is rising and number sold is falling, then demand could be falling. An average/balanced market may have a supply percentage of around 1.5–2.5%.

Average Vendor Discount

This is the difference between the asking price and the price the property is sold for. Vendor discounting is a similar measure to days on market in terms of sentiment in that market. If the vendor does not want to negotiate much in dropping the price (specific vendors aside, as some are just plain stubborn or disconnected from reality), then this is more of a seller's market and sellers can more likely get what they want. Bargains are less likely; this is a market where there is demand and potentially less supply, which is an indicator of capital growth.

Be careful that the location is not at its peak, because if it is, you are possibly better off waiting a few months and trying to buy somewhere you can negotiate more. If vendors are offering larger discounts, then it is a sign that this is an area to be cautious with, where there may be more supply than demand. However, consider that there may be an opportunity for a bargain.

In some states, vendors will sell below the list price, whilst in others, some of the estate agents have had a history of misleading the public by advertising properties at a lower price which would often sell for 10% over or much more. The higher the vendor discount, the more it is a buyer's market, and sellers are more prepared to or have to negotiate the price down. As the Average Vendor Discount figure approaches 10%, it is becoming a buyer's market. If the figure is below five, then it is more of a seller's market. Remember to look at the trend; the market could be overheated and have a correction, so it does not necessarily represent a good opportunity.

Property Cycle Position

Different locations are in different cycles. Each market is different; there are suburb markets within state markets, and then there are smaller markets within each suburb market based on property type, location within the suburb, and price point.

Demographics

Within a few years, generation X and Y will make up over 65% of the workforce, so the average age of the people living within a suburb is something to bear in mind. In other words, you need to consider buying a property that will be in demand for the specific demographic (e.g. Generation X, Y, or baby boomers) in the area. The older the demographic, the more likely they may want to downsize. Younger singles tend to want smaller dwellings, while young families prefer a house or large townhouse. Properties near employment hubs will be popular for a younger demographic. Baby boomers will soon be retired/retiring, and there will be a rising trend towards a sea or country change location, or downsizing to townhouses and units. Note that not every sea or country location will be popular, though.

To learn more about the people living in a suburb, you can easily access data on gender, religion, education level, marital status, languages spoken, employment types and industries, country of origin, and income levels from the Australian Bureau of Statistics. Remember, the more amenities, transport, education facilities, and other services, the more desirable a suburb is to live in and the more capital growth potential it has.

Suburbs that are more 'white collar' are better for growth. The residents earn more, their income generally rises at a greater rate, they can afford more debt or to pay more rent, and most importantly, they are less affected by economic downturns than 'blue collar' suburbs. An increase in white collar workers in an area is a good sign of capital growth to come, on the back of gentrification.

Gentrification, Income Levels, and Wage Growth

These are some of the most important factors to consider when choosing a suburb. If wages are not increasing and incomes are low, rents and prices will struggle to rise. Gentrification of a suburb, therefore, is something that can positively impact on the future capital growth and rents in the area. If you get in early, it can be a boon. The risk is if you miscalculate the rate at which a suburb is becoming more gentrified. A great example of a suburb which became an excellent property investment decision was in Williamstown, Victoria, where many years ago, investors were paying (on average) 300K for a house, compared to $1.8 million now.

Online Search Interest

The amount of online interest in a suburb, represented by 'low,' 'average,' or 'high.' This supports a decision on one suburb over another.

Rental Demand

Rental demand is also represented by 'low,' 'average,' or 'high,' and is also worth taking on board to gauge activity.

Building Activity

The more activity with development, the more supply there is, and the less capital growth there is in these growth corridors. Marketing companies use the term 'growth corridor' as a misleading indicator of a good investment area, and most people fall for it.

Proportion of Renters

Stability and desirability are key. A 30–35% proportion of renters may represent a more balanced market, on the basis that across Australia, roughly 33% of people rent, 33% possess their own property, and 33% have a mortgage on a property.

If the proportion of renters is over 40%, a concern could be that the area becomes downtrodden, where houses and gardens are not as well maintained compared to owner-occupied properties. It becomes less appealing for owner-occupiers to live there, so the resale market (and, in turn, capital growth prospects) can be more limited.

House and unit building approvals in an area, the dwelling supply comparative to forecasted population growth, and the current and projected future investor and home-buyer activity will come to bear on a suburb. New estates are confronted by these risks, and investors purchasing house and land packages or off-the-plan apartments face higher risks of supply outweighing demand.

This is the root issue I have with property marketing companies. An area may be good, but they typically pay little to no regard for the sheer supply of dwellings being built and sold in an area. There could be dozens of builders and developers flogging their wares in any given outer lying suburb, reducing the potential for short- to medium-term capital growth and increasing the risk that the projected rental income will not be achieved because too many investors will be trying to rent their properties out at the same time.

There will be higher risk of competition when trying to sell your property in the future if the estate in which you purchase has significant stock, especially in high rise, high density apartment blocks. You will then have a more significant chance of being forced to drop your price to improve the chances of selling your property, and therefore, you could make less capital growth.

Median Price

This is the middle of the market, meaning that 50% of properties in the area are under the median price and 50% are over. Median price can be a deceptive gauge. With second hand stock, you have more of an opportunity to negotiate with the seller. Sometimes buyers think that if they can buy their home or investment under median price then they are doing well.

Often, the contrary is the case. It is not enough just to buy in a good suburb; it is important to buy in a good street within that suburb. The best streets outperform the average and certainly the worst streets in terms of selling price. If you try to buy in a better pocket of a suburb, or a better dwelling than the average, you would expect to pay above median price for that property.

Be very careful, also, of a false median. When new stock in an area comes onto the market or land has been carved up with two or three townhouses built on it, this can lead to sales of property in the area with prices way above the median. These sales prices can lead novice buyers to believe there has been significant capital growth in the area when, in fact, prices may not have even risen.

What could have happened is one of many things; a newer property has sold for more than an older property, a larger property has been sold, more houses have been sold than townhouses or units, or larger parcels of land or development sites may have been sold. The median price can come back by a third or half in one month, then double in another.

Therefore, one should never rely on the median price for one more very important reason: the suburb is comprised of different sized dwellings. Size can be:

- *Number of bedrooms*
- *Size of each bedroom*
- *Number of living areas*
- *Number of bathrooms*
- *Size of land*
- *Garage versus carport*
- *Quality of inclusions*
- *Renovated versus unrenovated*

At a bare minimum, only ever use the median price of similarly sized dwellings to the one you are trying to buy as a starting point. Never use the median for the suburb. Compare apples with apples, in other words.

Marketing companies or developers selling off-the-plan properties do not customarily negotiate on price. There will be more on new versus established properties later in the book.

Hedonic Pricing

Using hedonic pricing to support decisions is more accurate than using the median house price. Hedonic pricing is used in several industries, and it is particularly useful in the real estate industry. Besides factoring in the neighbourhood, level of crime, proximity to amenities, transport and good/zoned schools, and the value of other properties in the area, it also takes into account the features, both internal and external, of a specific property (e.g. the inclusions, layout, aspect, size of the block of land and how flat it is, appearance … anything related to the property that will influence the price).

Of course, the suburb has a significant impact. For example, there may be a five-bedroom, five-bathroom house in a suburb with a median price of 400K, but the property may sell for a large margin below or above the median.

Whilst the median is not an accurate measure for the specific property, it does influence prices in general, because the price could still be significantly lower or higher than the same house in a much better/worse suburb.

The median price must be considered when researching at a suburb and specific property level, but it should not be relied on without considering the hedonic pricing method of determining a specific property's value and what you may have to pay for it.

Buying the best property in the worst suburb is dumb. Logic prevails when reversing this comment – buy the worst house in the best street – yet so many people make mistakes by building a mansion in a crappy suburb. This does not positively influence the capital growth of the property as much as buying a humbler dwelling in a much better suburb.

Pricing a property is reasonably straightforward, as it is based on available data and the market prices in the area. Like any data, hedonic pricing is not perfect.

Whilst it is based on what someone is willing to pay for the property, based on their perception of the benefits and disadvantages of the individual property, it can (on occasion) fail to acknowledge or recognise external influences on the price, such as interest rates, consumer sentiment, changes in regulations, or disruptive and noisy construction of other properties going on around it.

You must look at lag and lead indicators. Choosing suburbs based on past performance is a good start but still not sufficient. The property cycle that it is in should be understood, and the reasons the suburb performed well and whether they may continue to drive growth in the area need to be assessed. Look at drivers pushing growth moving forward, not just factors that have pushed growth in the past. These factors may be the same or similar, but this needs to be confirmed.

Leading indicators

- *GDP*
- *Population growth*
- *A trend line*
- *Employment growth*

Stay away from areas with job losses and companies closing down. A suburb with diverse industries can support and better absorb some job contraction.

Lag Indicators

Any data looking at what has happened is a lag indicator. The past is not a reliable indicator of the future, so lag indicators are not reliable on their own. They form part of the picture. You need to include lead indicators, trend directions of data, and more predictive data to complement the data representing the past.

Specific Property

This section will include a considerable amount of information relevant to finding a specific property, after you have shortlisted a suburb to focus on. You have considered your finances, budget, goals, and strategies. You have decided whether you will purchase a unit, townhouse, or house. You have chosen the strategy you wish to use, such as buy and hold or renovate or flip, and also if it will be capital growth or cash flow focused. You have chosen the state it will be in, and whether it is in the city, middle to outer suburbs, or a regional location.

Property Type

The property type should suit the majority of the demographic within a suburb. Buying a property that is smaller than those that suit the demographic can provide excellent opportunities to extend the dwelling to, say, a three-bedroom house, if that is the most suitable for the largest demographic segment. Sometimes adding a second living area, a third and fourth bedroom, or a second bathroom can significantly increase resale value and rental appeal.

Property Size

This can influence finance approvals, demand for resale and rental, and the future and current needs of the demographic of the area.

Each property has its own attributes, such as land size, Walk Score, size of rooms, number of rooms other than bedrooms, number of bathrooms, number of car spaces/parking, flat versus sloping land, inclusions (such as air conditioning), or the quality of fixtures and fittings. These all contribute to the assessment of a property and its hedonic price. Some buyers may ignore all of this if the price is attractive, but they do so to their own detriment.

For example, a client came to me already owning a small apartment in Sydney. It had no air conditioning, and no way of installing an air conditioning unit because the body corporate did not allow for a unit to be attached on the outside of the building.

This was a bit impractical to begin with, because the apartment was on the twenty-fifth floor as well. The apartment was not the best investment they could had made.

Walk Score

This is a score given to a property, between 0–100, as to its walkability to amenities. This can be important information in an area where people prefer to walk or get public transport. It can be less important in more regional locations, as people are generally used to driving.

Median Price for Dwelling Size

Stick to within 15–25% of this figure to not overcapitalise on the area, but also to buy in a better pocket or afford a better property.

Comparable Sales

Search for data on previous sales within the area; the more recent and similar to the specific property, the more reliable they are. Banks will normally undertake a valuation; either a valuer will visit the property, or it could be a drive by viewing or a desktop (computer generated) valuation. Valuers always use comparable sales to support their estimated value. Valuers may value a property down if they cannot source adequate or suitable comparable sales.

Whilst they may consider your purchased property to be worth what you have paid, they may not give it that value on paper, and this will mean you have to put in more of your own money. The risk of this happening more often occurs when buying a house and land package, and much more still when buying an off-the-plan apartment (I would estimate more than half the time).

On house and land packages, often a valuer will indicate the replacement insurance value to be greater than the value of the fixed price build contract. The replacement value for insurance purposes may contradict the valuation of the property for a number of reasons: lack of comparables, assumed future cost of rebuilding, the valuer does not think it is worth what you are paying, or in some instances the valuer may simply not like the property.

The buyer should at least get a computer-generated valuation done in order to guide you on what it may be worth paying for the property. Of course, a valuation can mean very little if there is a feeding frenzy at an auction. Maybe the next wave of Asian buyers has come, like what has happened to the Melbourne market.

Suburbs like Glen Waverley, Balwyn, Box Hill, Blackburn, and even all the way out beyond Ringwood have seen a wave of Asian activity. They want to buy where the rest of their community has, and there are some popular school zones which have led to inexplicable growth.

Rent Appraisal

By phoning rental managers, you can obtain an opinion on the tenant demand and desirability of certain pockets and streets, and the popularity of the different types of dwellings in a suburb. If houses are more popular, it is beneficial to know whether two living areas versus one living area, two bathrooms versus one bathroom, a garage versus carport, or off-street versus on-street parking is more in demand.

The size of each room, amount of storage, layout, functionality, floorplan, age, repairs risk, renovations cost, amount of depreciation, and inclusions all make a difference. These questions can be asked of sales agents from other agencies, who are not involved in the sale of the property, to give you confidence of the potential resell ability. I do not ever rely on the opinion of the sales agent in isolation, but I look for a consensus from other agents to support a decision.

Some property sellers may say to buy a simpler property with lower cost inclusions, so there is a lower cost to replace something if it is damaged by a tenant. Others will argue to spend more, so the property has owner-occupier appeal, but then there is some risk of overcapitalising.

A balance must be struck where you do not spend too much, especially in the case of an investment property. You are not going to live there, and your personal taste is irrelevant and potentially unappealing to others. Go for good quality, but not the best and not luxurious. Choose neutral colours with tiles, walls, curtains, and carpets to appeal to a wider demographic. Search for low maintenance gardens, as tenants cannot be expected to manage a flower garden.

House and Land

Everyone agrees that land appreciates and buildings depreciate, but a well-bought unit can potentially outperform an averagely bought house. The land value as a component of the purchase price has a bearing as well. It is unfortunate, though, that in an effort to buy a house on a block of land, you can come unstuck. Many house and land packages, or newly built houses in the outer suburbs where there is a larger supply of land available compared to closer in to the CBD, are on increasingly smaller blocks, edging towards 300 sq. m. Some townhouses, closer to more established areas, have more land than that. Whilst some outer areas are nice to raise a family and are worth investing in, not all of them are. As I mentioned earlier, some units, boutique apartments, and townhouses that are more central and popular for older and younger generations alike, not just family demographics, may be better investments.

It is wise to define what a unit is as well. It is a free-standing, single-storey dwelling. It is not part of a building, has no lift or communal stairwell, is on its own block of land, and is sometimes adjoining another unit or two. These are in shorter supply than apartments.

Older apartments, in smaller boutique developments of under twenty, have more character. They are often better built, have higher ceilings, and have more land value on title than newly built apartments. Developers, in my experience, can cut corners to save a dollar. Some smaller apartment developments have more land on title, because if there are three floors compared to thirty floors, for example, there are fewer apartments that share the same footprint. Off-the-plan issues associated with higher rise or high-density developments include lower land value per apartment, the owner-occupier percentage can often be out of whack with the investor percentage, and finance is more difficult to obtain.

Avoid niche properties; these will have fewer buyers interested. Lenders may lend less, which means you waste more of your own money, having to inject more towards the purchase. Resell ability, owner-occupier appeal, and ease of finance all play a part in the process, so typical things to avoid include converted warehouses, apartments above shops, student accommodation, high rise/high density apartments, apartments under 50 sq. m, serviced apartments, stratum or company share titles, studios, farming zoned properties, or green wedges and hobby farms.

Too many people have purchased through spruikers in unsustainable regional areas based on hype, in regions such as Queensland, northern Western Australia, one-horse towns, or low population regional hubs. The sheer volume of supply, due to being plagued by developers and property marketing companies, has led investors to fail in droves.

Do not invest too heavily in a coastal town, far from civilisation. Coastal towns will see a lot of stock on the market, as many holiday homes will be sold through necessity. They are the first properties to go. People shed their materialistic add-ons which they accumulated during the good times. Many people get carried away, and do not consider the future cost of debt.

Consider limiting what you invest in regional towns as well, especially in the case of Queensland. Regional towns in Queensland have less going for them, particularly from a transport perspective. Queensland has always been the poor cousin of New South Wales and Victoria when considering the Eastern seaboard for investment, and has continually failed to perform. Whilst there are some excellent locations in Queensland worth investing in, most areas are a flash in the pan.

New or an Established Property?

Benefits of New Property

- *If you wish to reduce risk of repairs and maintenance, then new is handier. The builder generally covers defects.*
- *Light and space are often maximised and more appealing to tenants. They are typically more energy efficient than a property which is thirty years older.*

- *From a tax point of view, they usually offer higher or longer depreciation benefits, not only from the fixtures and fittings, but also from capital works. Investors can use these tax benefits to assist with annual or potentially monthly cash flow.*
- *Potential stamp duty savings*
- *Potential greater tenant appeal.*

Disadvantages of New Property

- *They often cost more than older properties in the same area. You pay a premium for the better technology that is included and you have a choice of inclusions.*
- *Too many similar properties could be promoted by property marketing companies in the same or nearby areas.*
- *Generally, you cannot negotiate on the contract price.*
- *Over-capitalising becomes a problem depending on what upgrades and inclusions are installed.*
- *Massive risk if you buy direct from the developer or through a property marketing company. You are better off using an intermediary that has access to many property portals and dozens of developments across Australia, which are not restricted to any one property seller and are not limited by property type, suburb location, or state.*
- *Cannot add value/renovate/subdivide, as someone has already benefited from that process.*

It is highly recommended that you consider avoiding off-the-plan contracts where you pay a 10% deposit and the remaining 90% when construction is completed.

Contracts where finance is not approved and settled after the approval can take twelve months to four years to complete. Your finance approval is less than useless, and valuations may not stack up in the future.

New Property Valuations

Factors that are not generally considered in a valuation for a new property include:

- *Level of finish or quality. Better quality means the construction contract price is higher, but a valuation may not reflect this.*
- *Comparable sales in the location within three months. I see some valuations under contract price in newer estates, because houses around them may be much older, and there can be fewer comparable sales.*
- *With investment property lending and interest-only lending being the subject of great scrutiny by APRA and the banks, no doubt the valuers feel that they will also be under pressure.*
- *Some valuers do not fully appreciate the property.*
- *Lenders are starting to instruct valuers to deduct GST from the sale price of new property, leading to the property being valued lower than the contract price.*
- *Site costs, like soil tests, fences, and blinds may not be fully recognised in the valuation.*

Benefits of Older Property

With older properties, there is a lot more variation when it comes to their condition and value, but there are still many advantages to consider.

- *Ability to negotiate*
- *You can potentially add instant value through renovating, extending, subdividing, and/or developing.*
- *Older properties are often situated on larger blocks, which can help drive property values upwards.*
- *Easier to find in well-established suburbs, which can demonstrate consistent growth.*

Disadvantages of Older Property

- *Cost of maintenance; if renovations are required to make the property more liveable, or more modern to attract better tenants, there could be a loss of rental income during the renovation period.*
- *Lower rental rates, higher maintenance costs, and lower depreciation would negatively impact on your monthly cash flow.*
- *Cannot depreciate fixtures and fittings for properties with contracts entered into after May 2017.*

An electrical and plumbing inspection for an older property is recommended, as well as a building inspection on any property. The electrical and plumbing inspection costs can vary significantly; on average they cost \$300–\$600. A property inspection could cost \$300–\$500. A pest inspection may cost around \$200–\$300.

When considering the amount of land in your investment purchase, it is well worth appreciating that the value per square metre of land can often be more important than the amount of land. It is possible to purchase 100 acres for under 300K, but it may take thirty years to double in value. In comparison, a unit on 200 sq. m of land in a blue chip suburb could double in value in seven years.

Buying a block of land perceived to be suitable for development may be hindered by overlays, lack of precedent in the area, easement, and – in Victoria – the new mandatory minimum allowance requirements for garden and green area on the land. These factors all play a part in due diligence and suitability. In Victoria, according to the Department of Environment, Land, Water and Planning, the garden area requirements are as follows:

- *Lot size 400–500 square metres requires a minimum garden area of 25%*
- *Lot size 501–650 square metres requires a minimum garden area of 30%*

- *Lot size > 650 square metres requires a minimum garden area of 35%*

Holding a property long enough needs to be sustainable; we need to live for today, tomorrow, and the future.

- *Interest rates, owners' corporation fees, rental increases, vacancy rates, your surplus income/savings, and any amount that can be saved in a redraw facility offsetting the interest repayments on a loan should all play a part in your decisions, and certainly your plan.*

The Australian dream is no longer a large suburban quarter acre block. Safety, lower crime, community, amenities, schools, and less travel time to employment and job opportunities are all key.

People are time poor, so a townhouse may be just as important to a family as a house if it has enough bedrooms and a small yard, at least. The generations on either side of Generation X favour townhouses, as do tenants, as they are low maintenance and allow people to live closer in to a CBD or major hubs at less of a purchase/rental price than a house.

For capital growth, the following factors can play a very important part:

- *The demographic of an area. Buy in an area that has a long history of strong capital growth and will continue to outperform the averages.*
- *Consider buying a property where capital growth can be manufactured through redeveloping the property or renovating it, rather than relying on and waiting for the market to provide capital growth.*
- *Land is a considerable component of the value of the property.*
- *Consider a property with some scarcity to it, due to it being more unique.*

Unit versus House

You cannot always compare the two as easily as you may like. The suburb in which the dwelling is located is what is important. After all your research, you can compare the performance of a suburb within your budget and the past growth of specifically sized dwellings very easily. Units, apartments, and townhouses often offer better proximity to amenities and transport, and are more affordable than a house in the same suburb. They have a higher rental yield, but this can be weighed down by the owners corporation fees. Some housing estates in master planned communities can be accompanied with owner management fees as well, so be aware.

Lower maintenance, smaller dwellings like units, apartments, and townhouses offer investors a way into the property market. They can have land worth more than the larger blocks that comes with a house, even if the land per square metre is smaller, depending on where it is and what it is being compared to. Never fall into the trap of believing the general statement that houses perform better than units.

The advantages of spending less on a unit, boutique apartment, townhouse, or regional area are:

- *Diversification*
- *Investor has less to lose if, by some chance, everything turned pear-shaped (always invest with the worst case in mind)*
- *Preserves equity/cash as a lower deposit is required*
- *Potentially able to invest in more and different markets, and take advantage of different property cycles*
- *It is a baby step – especially if this is your first go.*
- *Yields are generally more attractive and the properties could pay for themselves.*

- *Lower stamp duty*
- *If you maximise the use of your borrowing capacity by spending it all on one property, it will be harder to buy more properties in the future, and therefore harder to grow a portfolio, so purchasing a smaller priced property can help toward preserving your available savings/equity for use toward another property.*

As a general rule, capital growth properties are normally found within 15 to 20km of the CBD. Of course, there are markets within markets. Capital growth can occur just as well in many other locations, but it can also come back significantly and crash. The more negatively geared properties, though, are often found in close proximity to Australia's capital cities, and rent is generally lower with these properties. Cash flow positive properties are located further out in the outer suburbs, bordering the edge of the metro areas, and in regional areas. Areas fraught with danger where cash flow is high are mining towns.

Despite the many choices out there – such as capital growth, cash flow, inner city, outer ring suburbs, regional, new, established, houses, villas, apartments, units, terraces, dual occupancies, and houses – ultimately, all residential property falls into two categories.

Category 1: To be Avoided (for investment)

For purposes of comparison, let's rule out the undesirables, for investment:

- *Serviced apartments*
- *Student accommodation*
- *Buildings with over seventy-five apartments*
- *Buildings with more than ten to fifteen apartments in a regional location*
- *Buildings with lifts*

- *Buildings with pools*
- *Resorts*
- *Dwellings under 50 sq. m living*
- *Land with too much fall/slope*
- *Apartments in large complexes in high density postcodes (e.g. 3000–3009 in Victoria).*
- *Properties with limitations built into the owners' corporation. Limitations and exclusions can affect the following things:*
    - Pets: May prevent you from allowing a tenant with a pet to stay there, which can limit the size of the rental market.
    - Parking: I have seen tenants (quite rudely and antisocially, I might add) use a visitor parking spot to park their car, their second car, or their girlfriend/ boyfriend's car which spends four nights a week at the property.
    - Parties: Understand the rules, and apply these to your tenants to avoid getting other owners/tenants offside.
    - Short-term lease restrictions can apply, eliminating you from renting out to short stay tenants, such as Airbnb tenants.
    - Improvements: You will be limited to what you can do. You may own the living space, but not the walls, car parking spot(s), or doors. You cannot add much value, if any, to an apartment.
    - Rogue management: potential increases in the owners' corporation fees is a risk

Other types of properties to avoid include busy roads, locations near high tension power lines, land with too much slope to build on in a cost-effective manner, uninsurable areas (due to flood, fire etc.), low population areas, and units with large owners' corporation costs (high costs mitigate any benefit from high yield).

Any off-the-plan contracts should be avoided if you are unsure about your job stability, and more importantly because lenders are constantly changing how much a person can borrow.

I see and hear of many people losing their deposits because they cannot settle, meaning that developers can retain the 10% deposit (perhaps amounting to 40–100K) and then on-sell the property to someone else. Often contracts prevent the buyer on-selling the property prior to settlement, so there is no way out!

Category 2: To be Considered (provided they do not fall within the previous points)

Units, apartments, townhouses, houses, villas, houses with a granny flat (more popular in New South Wales), and dual income properties (very popular in Queensland, and growing in popularity in New South Wales) should all be considered. In light of economic instability, rising interest rates for investment lending, tightening of credit policy, managing exposure to the risk of future cost of debt, recognition of the risk of less capital growth in the future, and many investors with loans soon converting to P&I from I/O, it is more important than ever to consider the future cost of debt and make allowances for this when weighing up cash flow versus capital growth.

Refer to my book *Property Investing Made Simple* for greater depth on the types of property to consider. I believe advice and research is only professional if it serves the person it is provided to. It should have nothing to do with any vested interests, belief systems, attitudes, or religion of the person who is providing the advice. If the advice/research provider is engaged by the vendor to promote/sell one property, location, or strategy over another, anything that comes out of their mouth under the pretext it is independent and objective is unprofessional and unethical.

Figure 9: Research Process

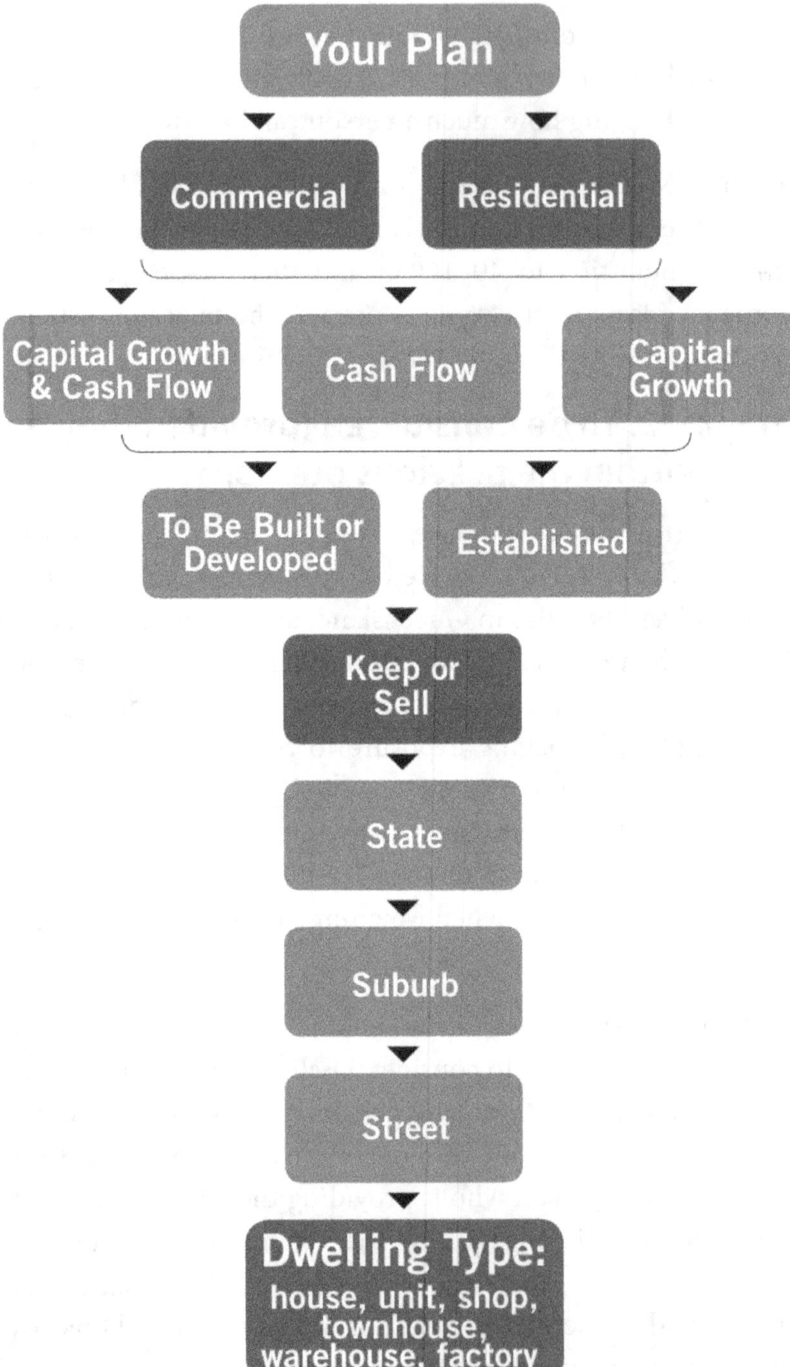

Is a Heritage Listed Property Worth Considering?

Overall, this depends on your budget, and your strategy. Heritage listed homes can often be found in expensive inner city suburbs, as they were built before the urban sprawl and have benefits in their proximity to the CBDs of capital cities. But is it their individual appeal that makes them a winner from a capital growth perspective, or is it, in fact, the area in which they lie that has created the value in these properties?

There are various types of property that may have a Heritage Overlay, such as Victorian, Federation, and Art Deco. Once we head into 70s- and 80s-style homes, charm and character have been watered down from earlier periods. Properties from this more recent era are typically not heritage entitled, but renovation opportunities do emerge to add value to these.

Formal designation of 'heritage' provides recognition and, in turn, preservation of the character, charm, and history of the property. Research suggests that there is more than an intrinsic value associated to a heritage listed property, from pride to capital growth benefits. According to the NSW Office of Environment and Heritage, "There is growing evidence to support the view that heritage listing has a positive impact on property values, and real estate advertisements are starting to reflect this." They also say it "is a source of pride for many people."

Often, buyers are apprehensive when considering a heritage property, which is often unwarranted, unless they are considering knocking it down, or subdividing and building next to it. Knocking it down is usually very difficult, sometimes nigh impossible, and subdividing to build one or more dwellings next door may cost significantly more due to heritage requirements (mainly regarding the façade). The land lacks the value it would otherwise have with a non-heritage property that could be subdivided. Some people try to renovate and restore these homes internally, but all too often they use inferior materials which are less ornate and, ultimately, they fail to even superficially add or preserve the original charm. Heritage properties can lose their charm and be devalued from internal changes done poorly. Some people successfully add a modern aspect to these homes, and it can be very nice walking through the historic part of the dwelling to the ultra-modern.

So, what makes a heritage home desirable? Perhaps it is the baltic pine floors, 14 ft. ceilings, timber skirting boards, ornate cornices, mortared solid walls, double brick, steep pitched roof, hydronic oil or water heating, double hung windows, solid doors, or hessian plaster rosettes? Not to mention the craftsmanship, design, charm, representation of an era, uniqueness, and scarcity. Victorian, Queen Anne, and Edwardian (also known as Federation) properties all have benefits, appeal, and unique design features.

Edwardian properties (1890–1915) draw on both Victorian and Queen Anne in their features, but they are less cluttered than Victorian. Some people favour the clutter, dark colours, and heaviness of Victorian properties, others the cheerful, refreshing Edwardian style. Certain studies suggest that Georgian may be the most popular style with its grandeur, although some real estate agents believe that Victorian-era properties are generally most in demand, with Edwardian close behind.

It depends who you ask as to what they prefer (some people prefer the modern era's stark geometry). For most people, owning a heritage listed property is entirely aspirational, as period homes are often in expensive areas. These homes represent our heritage; a precious resource providing an identity and distinctiveness to an era, community, or culture. Time has shown that properties with these appeals, which benefit from being different and scarce, have weathered downturns in the market, which is not surprising when they are compared to dime a dozen properties around them and in the outer suburbs.

It is not all rosy, though. Maintenance and upkeep can be higher in cost. These dwellings can be more difficult to heat internally, and possess strict requirements as to colour schemes and types of fencing. Retaining the façade (what is visible to the street) is the obvious factor. Comparable sales are potentially lacking; however, valuers tend to underpin a heritage property with its own intrinsic value that other properties lack.

The owner must seek approval from the council to alter the elements of the property that give reason for its heritage designation. It is these elements that the buyer should understand. The biggest mistake is not undertaking enough due diligence when purchasing. Often it is owner-occupiers that outbid investors, due to a strong willingness to maintain such a property for prosperity's sake, personal pride, and differentiation.

Considerations that influence why an investor may be interested in purchasing a property with a heritage overlay can include the fact that these properties are usually in blue chip, inner city suburbs, benefiting from consistent capital growth. These investors are not looking for cash flow and they will not get it from heritage properties. Tenants normally prefer internally maintained properties, unlike many heritage properties. Ultimately, assume 80% of capital growth is contributable to the suburb and location within the suburb, and 20% to the dwelling itself. The power of the remaining 20% associated with the dwelling possibly has more weight associated to it, due to its uniqueness.

Today, properties are built using inferior materials, such as MDF skirting boards (rather than timber), plaster board for walls (not solid render), foam cornices, hollow doors, and cheap hinges, not to mention a complete lack of character, craftsmanship, uniqueness, and charm. Corners are being cut for affordability and economies of scale.

Overall, the restrictions over the Heritage Overlay may vary greatly, depending on zoning, other overlays in the area, and the extent of the heritage recognition. Heritage properties can be beneficial for an owner-occupier and investor alike, but can also be prohibitive in price and changes to the property are often more expensive.

The individual's personal goals, risk profile, risk appetite, and investment strategy should be taken into account prior to considering purchasing a heritage property. A range of factors, such as services and amenities in and around an area, the quality of individual properties, the suitability of the property for the demographic, lot sizes, prevailing trends in the market cycle, and zoning all affect the prices and growth of both heritage and non-heritage properties. It is fair to say that the longer one holds onto an asset which is already scarce, over time, it will become scarcer. In property, scarcity is a capital growth driver.

Capital Growth versus Cash Flow Properties

This topic is high on the radar of most investors. The answer is often not straightforward. Good capital growth locations typically have low to medium yield. This means the property would likely be negatively geared. Cash flow focused properties are in areas with less capital growth, and can be positive cash flow properties depending not just on rent and interest rates, but also on costs. At least cash flow strategy reduces the risk of being exposed too much to the unknown future cost of debt. Fixing rates can help as well, but mainly in the short term.

Many investors would like a capital growth property, but do not want the property to negatively impact on their lifestyle. Well, there is no perfect property. Compromises must be made. A positive cash flow property can assist in reducing the mortgage on the borrower's principal place of residence (PPR), which in turn creates more equity. This has a compounding effect on the reduction of the mortgage, so hopefully in the near future, the borrower can focus on reducing any investment debt split against the PPR, (note; a loan split represents part of the total loan secured against the property, splitting the loan enables the borrower to have part of the loan on a variable rate or part on a fixed rate, which could include part of the loan on interest only and part on principle and interest. It also seperates investment purpose debt from owner occupier purpose debt, handy for your accountant).

One cannot just focus on cash flow properties, either, as wealth creation stems from capital growth, not cash flow. Just focusing on cash flow also works against a purchaser by eating into their equity in their home for the money to pay as a deposit towards the purchase of an investment property, rather than tapping into any growing equity in their investment properties. This leaves them less able to purchase more properties (because they have run out of cash or equity).

Whilst a borrower can borrow more money based on servicing (their capacity to afford debt according to the calculator used by the lender), they may not have the deposit and costs accessible in cash or equity to put towards a new property. Until banks start lending 100% of the purchase price plus stamp duty (which will probably never happen), investors should build a portfolio based on both cash flow and capital growth.

The risk with too much of a capital growth strategy is the amount the borrower could be out of pocket while holding the property, and in a rising interest rate market, the risk grows. There is no point buying a capital growth focused property if there is a clear and present risk that in the near future the property needs to be sold. You might experience job uncertainty, tightening lending policies, lower borrowing capacity, and the risk of being a slave to the property, and the risk of having to sell it due to unforeseen circumstances is much higher. Any changes to negative gearing could also be problematic. Borrowing less, by putting in more of the investor's own money, means the property becomes more neutrally geared, but not every investor has the luxury of committing larger amounts of equity to the one property.

There are several considerations to bear in mind to determine which option, out of a capital growth option and a higher cash flow option, could be better, such as the future combined. It would be too easy, and very wrong, to base a decision on the below outcomes alone, though. There are several other considerations to bear in mind to determine which option could be better, such as the future cost of debt, tax deductions, and affordability. One may cost of debt, tax deductions, and affordability. The wrong choice of option may cost several thousand dollars a year, potentially making the purchaser a slave to the debt. The other may provide several thousand dollars in income, assisting in not only holding the property, but also reducing any debt against the investor's principal place of residence.

If someone wants to grow a well-sized portfolio, they need to consider having a balance of capital growth and cash flow properties.

Timing, as to when you should use a cash flow strategy or a capital growth strategy, is one of the most important elements to a plan. Armed with the advice from the right property advisor, a plan, and some well-thought-out strategies, an investor could reduce the risk of running out of servicing capacity or equity.

Money In and Money Out

Income

Rental income in dollar terms can be converted to a yield percentage based on the annual rent divided by the value of the property. For example, if deciding whether to purchase a 400K investment property, it is wise to understand the yield, not just the rental dollar figure. So, if the property earns $340 a week, this equates to $18,200 p.a.

Divide $18,200 by $400,000 then multiply by 100, which equals a 4.55% yield (gross).

Besides stamp duty, there are other costs associated with purchasing an investment property.

Interest on the Mortgage

This is possibly the biggest variable, except during the term of a fixed rate. Lenders are constantly changing their rates independent of the RBA, especially for investment loans or interest-only loans. This became common after mid-2015, and prevalent in 2016.

Property Management Fees

This is a percentage of the rental income derived from the investment property. It can vary per state, but a reasonable average to use is between 6% and 8% plus GST. Sometimes this figure can be negotiated down to 5% plus GST. In more regional areas, where perhaps there are limited agents who may know each other well and communicate behind the scenes to reduce the chances of competition, they can get away with demanding an 11% fee. An example of a location where some people like to invest but fees are high is Broken Hill, New South Wales. To understand what a good property manager should be expected to do, refer to my book *Property Investing Made Simple.*

Letting and Advertising Fees

Managing agents charge a fee to let the investment property, and later on, re-let the property, even if the same tenant stays on for a further twelve months.

Council Rates

Whilst the tenant pays for usage, the landlord must pay for the facility, such as water and council rates. Sometimes, water is part of council rates. Rates in different states vary.

Insurance

This can entail only landlord insurance, or building insurance as well. Typically, the only time there may be no need for building insurance is if there is an owners' fee being charged. This fee covers the building insurance in most circumstances. The main inclusions in a landlord insurance policy must be:

- *If the tenant defaults, that loss of rent is covered.*
- *Cover of vandalism or malicious damage, by the tenants or their guests*
- *Burglary or theft by the tenant's guests or the tenant themselves.*

Other things that should be considered include liability insurance for injury to the tenant and to their guests (invited or not invited) and rental loss caused by insured events, such as fires, flooding, or other forces of nature, depending where the property is.

For example, in Darwin, you would require additional insurance for weather events. There are other costs to consider, such as legal costs of evicting the tenant, tax audits fees, locks needing to be changed, and re-letting expenses.

Repairs and Maintenance

It cannot be assumed that these will never occur; in fact, it is more likely than not that they will occur (less so with a new property, unless the builder is terrible).

I have seen a case where a builder scammed all of the people who worked for him. Then he left the country, and the driveway started to crack. This was not included in the client's landlord or building insurance policy. The builder's insurance provider did not want to cover it, and the council were not interested in knowing about it.

The older the property, the less is covered by any original insurance or warranty provided by the builder. Normally, after seven years, nothing is covered.

In an older property, it is more likely that things will need replacing. Some big ticket items may be a split system cooling and heating unit, hot water service, and evaporative cooling, then internal features like carpeting, window furnishings, and tiles.

Owners' Corporation

This fee can range from as little as $1,000 p.a. to over $5,000 p.a. In Cairns, Townsville, and Darwin, some of the owners' corporation fees are over $5,000. In buildings with lifts, swimming pools, gardens, and gated entrances, or resort-style buildings, body corporate fees can be over $4,000. Be careful to do your due diligence on apartments or villas, as the owners' corporation can seriously undermine the (often higher) rental associated with them.

Land Tax

This does not affect every investor, as it depends on which state you buy in, how many properties you have, and which entity you buy the property in. It is based on the land value of the property, not the dwelling on the land. An apartment may only have 10% of its value as land if it is new, 20% for a new unit, 30% for a new townhouse, and 40–50% for a new house. This percentage grows, as a percentage of the value, as the building depreciates on the land. This goes for all properties. A land tax bill will always rise unless, perhaps, you buy in an area you should not have.

CHAPTER 5

Buyer's Agent (The Help You Must Have)

There are three choices a person has when buying property

1. *Risk getting it wrong by doing all the work themselves*
2. *Use someone who represents the seller*
3. *Use a buyer's agent*

Why Use a Buyer's Agent/Advocate to Help Purchase Your Property?

When someone is looking to buy a property, whether it is an owner-occupied or investment property, they typically deal with a real estate agent. While those people may feel that the agent is showing them the property and helping them out, the agent is really working to maximise the sale price (which is counter to what the buyer wants). To rely on a real estate agent in a transaction where the agent is representing the seller is against the buyer's interests in every way, shape, and form.

A buyer's agent represents the buyer, not the seller. A good buyer's agent protects their client from bias and subjective opinions provided by real estate agents and property marketing companies. A buyer's advocate or buyer's agent, in the true sense, acts on behalf of the buyer to source a property. They are independent of the property, not engaged or employed by the seller, whereas a real estate agent essentially works for the vendor and is not independent of the property. They may be very friendly to the buyer, and answer many questions, but anyone who is employed to sell property cannot look after a buyer properly. They have a vested interest in the property and they cannot ethically or otherwise represent the buyer in the same transaction.

It is a little bit like comparing a mortgage broker to a bank. When someone walks into a bank, the only products that bank can offer are that bank's products; whereas, a mortgage broker can offer products from a range of lenders.

A real estate agent is looking to sell the property, or only properties within their agency, whereas the buyer's agent sources and shortlists a variety of available properties around the state (or country) which meet the brief provided by the buyer and/or are recommended by the buyer's agent. Most importantly, these are properties that the buyer's agent has not been engaged to sell or market by the vendor.

Some buyer's agents merely source what the buyer wants, normally for owner-occupying purposes. Another type of buyer's agent guides the buyer as to where and what the buyer should consider purchasing in more of an advisory process.

There is a brief; shorter in terms of what the buyer has asked for, but just as long, if not longer, in terms of the boxes it should tick to be a good investment opportunity.

The foundation of the brief will contain the maximum purchase price and strategy the property should conform to (such as cash flow or capital growth), which could then lead to whether their desired property is inner city, middle to outer ring metro, or regional. The location may be the determining factor on whether the investor pursues a new or established property as a best fit for price, demographic, and valuation, or both choices may be equally suitable.

Some clients may want established so the property can be rented out immediately, while others want to reduce stamp duty and increase depreciation.

Each buyer's needs are assessed separately to the next.

Many people are time poor and need someone to help with the legwork to find a property that meets their needs. They do not have the time to go to open houses every weekend. They do not have time to go to auctions or learn the rules of the game at an auction.

They may fear that their emotion will take over at an auction, causing them to bid above the amount they should. The buyer will normally lack the knowledge and experience the buyer's agent has (do your due diligence on your buyer's agent to ascertain this).

It is important for each buyer to seek out the services of someone who will look after them personally, educate them, and shelter them from the games that real estate agents and property marketing companies will play (particularly the non-disclosure regularly practiced by property marketing companies as to commissions and bonuses that they will earn by promoting any property).

A buyer's agent helps those time poor people with research, sourcing, attending auctions, attending open houses, doing the legwork, and negotiating on the buyer's behalf. A good buyer's agent is typically better at negotiating than a buyer is, because they do it regularly, which means the buyer's agent can potentially save the buyer a considerable amount of money.

What Makes a Good Buyer's Agent?

An okay buyer's agent follows the brief. They go out and find what the client is looking for. This is excellent for an owner-occupier, provided the agent is experienced, and qualified. For example, a client may want a four-bedroom house with a swimming pool in Hawthorn, Victoria as an investment property.

The buyer's agent may find that property on the right sized block, with the right sized bedrooms, and maybe even painted in the right colours. However, they may ignore things like whether or not it is on a busy road, whether it is near high tension power lines, whether it is near an industrial area, or even whether it is priced above the median price. This buyer's agent may just try to find the property the client wants, rather than considering the size, the proximity to all necessary infrastructure, and the location.

On the other hand, a good buyer's agent does not simply follow the brief. A good buyer's agent attempts to guide the client to what they should consider, rather than simply finding what the client thinks they need. This type of agent is aware of what properties to avoid.

A good buyer's agent, in my opinion, should guide the client away from considering a serviced apartment, student or studio accommodation, a high-rise, high-density apartment, or an apartment with under 50 sq. m of living space. He/she helps take into account things that the buyer has not thought about. After all, their clients may know what they want, but they might not know what is best for them.

It is easy to distinguish a buyer's agent that is not very good. They lose touch with the market, especially if all they focus on is owner-occupiers.

Buyer's agents who focus on investors pay attention to trends in data. Good agents avoid hype, hearsay, and opinion, and look for trends in several different data points, including median price, growth over twelve months and the last five/ten years, time on the market, capital growth, yield, vacancy rates, stock on market, and supply and demand. A good buyer's agent also drills down to street level.

An average buyer's agent is just an order taker. They may not follow the brief properly, or they shortlist properties that only meet some of the client's stated criteria. Perhaps he/she is lazy and cannot be bothered spending the necessary time to find more appropriate properties. Many do not have the required financial knowledge they should, and they may not consider things that would adversely affect the buyer's ability to apply for finance.

At a bare minimum, a buyers' agent should have obtained, as a bear minimum, the qualification of 'agent's representative' (an agent's representative is someone who has not continued on with further education to obtain their full real estate agent's license, but they have undertaken some level of study). However, it is better to deal with a fully licensed agent (even better if the undertake the required qualifications to become licensed in more than one state). . To add even more value to the client, they should not only be insured to perform the duties of a buyer's agent, but also have insurance that covers him/her to give advice.

Property Advice

In a regulated market, it is easier to tick boxes (meet a recognized industry standard or benchmark) in order to be recognized as entitled to purchase professional indemnity insurance.

In an unregulated market, there are not any boxes to tick. You have to demonstrate a very compliant, ethical, buyer-centric model, complete with fee disclosure and follow a code of conduct, in order to be entitled to give advice. It is the difference between earning an entitlement, rather than simply ticking a box with the expectation that you are going to receive an entitlement.

Never deal with a buyer's agent or property investment advisor if they do not have professional indemnity insurance. Whilst this insurance is to protect the advisor (every person or company operating in a professional/regulated environment does, or should have professional indemnity insurance), it demonstrates that the advisor is considered worthy to have insurance, by an insurance provider. If someone does not have insurance, they may not be able to get it, perhaps due to not being considered a good operator or worthy to have it, in the eyes of the insurer.

A good property advisor should also be a PIPA (Property Investment Professionals of Australia) member. PIPA is a group that provides education, a benchmark of qualifications, and barriers to entry for any advisor wishing to join their ranks.

They also practice a code of conduct that any property advisor, if they are good, will adhere to. Going a step further, a good property advisor would be a qualified property investment advisor (QPIA), in addition to being a member of PIPA.

Property advice has to come from a property advisor – not from a financial planner, mortgage broker, nor accountant, in the same way that financial planners cannot provide mortgage advice under their financial planning licence.

The need for professional property investment advice services that are buyer-centric is, and has been a rapidly growing and vitally important industry for property investors. The need for this service has come about because of the rise in the number of people selling properties that are not licensed, that are not insured, that represent the seller and masquerade around pretending to represent the buyer (wolves in sheep clothing). .

ASIC does not recognise property as an investment security. The most a financial planner can do is allow some asset allocation towards property as an asset class.

A financial planner cannot help you develop a financial plan that includes advice for a specific property. A good financial planner, if they are not suitably qualified, will point you in the direction of a buyer's agent or property advisor.

SPECIALIST ADVISORS

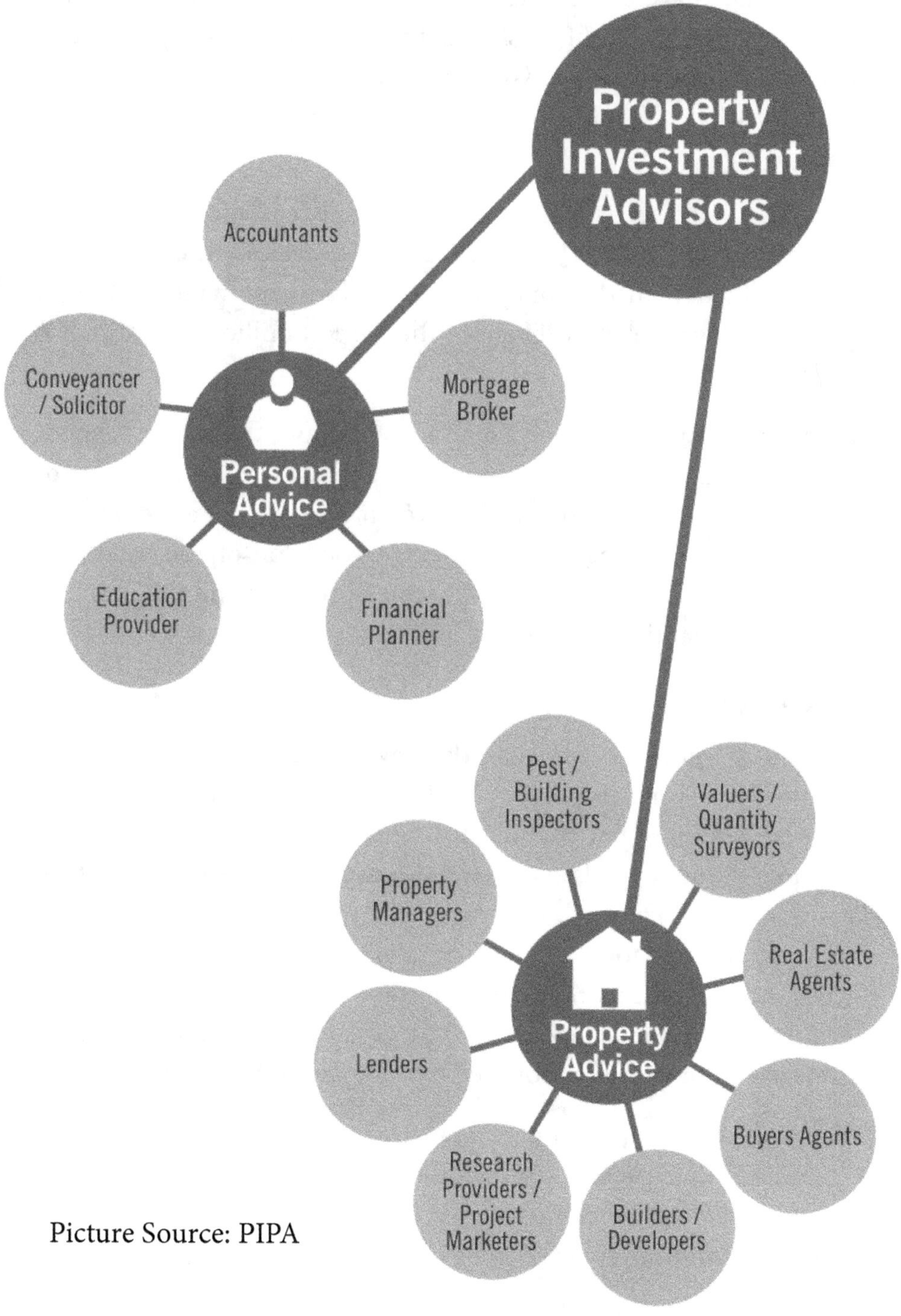

Picture Source: PIPA

Property investment advisors, operating solely as property advisors or buyer's agents, can only deal with property, not shares or insurances (unless they have a financial services licence). A property advisor looks at your risk profile, risk appetite, goals, and they complete a fact find on you to look at your assets, liabilities, and income. They hash out what is suitable in respect to your job security, health, age, and goals.

A property advisor is as important as a financial planner, because property is one of the best ways to build wealth. After all, most people who have made money in their lifetime have made it through property. A greater percentage of the world's millionaires are into property, not shares.

Some financial planners have dual accreditations that allow them to put on another hat as a property advisor, because they may be insured and may be a PIPA member. However, if they are not a member of PIPA or PIAA (Property Investment Association of Australia), or they are not insured to provide advice on property, and they are not disclosing what they are earning, walk away.

Fees

Obviously, someone who has this level of expertise is going to require a fee. Some people see a big fee, and get worried. They should be more fearful of not paying a fee, because you normally get what you pay for. It depends on what you want and what you expect to get in return. Take food, for example. Some people just want to go to a popular fast food chain. That is all well and good; you know what you are getting. Some people want fine dining, or they want healthier foods, and they are going to spend more money for that. You have to shop around for the price you are willing to pay.

It is similar to paying a financial planner to create a plan; that is a no brainer because that planner could make that fee back for you many times over by saving money on your property. A very good buyer's agent or a property advisor can guide you towards a better location to invest in than what you might have chosen yourself. They can also help with finding a property that has a lower risk, therefore saving you money on repairs, maintenance, location problems, issues applying for a loan, and more. Furthermore, when you go into a transaction with an experienced negotiator going to bat on your behalf, there is a greater likelihood that they will save you money in that transaction.

Many people buy a car with little forethought. They buy a lounge suite without any consideration other than its colour, comfort, cost, and whether it fits in the room. When you are buying a property, as much as you can, you want to reduce the risk of making any mistakes. Just one can cost you several hundreds of thousands of dollars. I think the figures speak for themselves. It makes sense to pay someone a few thousand dollars to help you reduce the risk of making a several hundred-thousand-dollar mistake. It is important to look at what you are getting to understand that the fee allows you to employ someone who will locate and interpret data in order to reduce risk. They do all the work for you in locating and researching property, so you do not have to lose time or money, nor be stressed in the process.

Some charge a fee in the form of a percentage, while others charge a fixed fee. I had one buyer's agent approach me to help him personally. He was in New South Wales and wanted my expertise for a particular suburb in Victoria. Whilst going through the process of engaging me, he explained that his own mother had paid a buyer's agent 2% on a one million dollar, one-bedroom apartment in Sydney. This, I must say, is quite expensive. Contact me to understand what is a reasonable fee.

Better than Free

There is a difference in what happens when you pay for expertise to when you go to some seminar expecting to receive something for free. When you go to one of these property marketing companies, you may not pay them anything at first. They will probably give you a beautiful, glossy brochure. For many people, it is very appealing to not have to pay anything, especially when it all looks so nice. What people do not think about is that they should not have to pay anything to deal with a person who represents the seller. People are drawn in by having something attractive offered to them, even when what is offered is not necessarily suitable for their personal situation.

If you want someone to help you make more potential capital growth or yield, and to reduce risk with your purchase, then do not deal with a property marketing company. If someone likes dealing with a company representative who typically does not disclose what they are earning, or the fact that they are employed by the developer/vendor, then great. They can go right ahead (I say this with a hint of sarcasm).

For some people, unfortunately, their fear of doing something is greater than their fear of doing nothing. These people may retire on the Government pension like over 80% of the population, and play bingo for the rest of their lives because they cannot afford anything else. Nothing against bingo, but for most people, it would be nice to have options.

On the other hand, sometimes people do get excited about really low interest rates and think, "Maybe it is time I overcome my 'coulda, woulda, shoulda' attitude, inaction, or procrastination, and actually do something." Then, they go out and buy from a spruiker or real estate agent, thinking that getting involved in the property market is all they need to focus on. The reality is that might be the worst thing they could do. It is great that they are going to buy property, but they need to give themselves the respect they deserve by trying to do it right. Regardless of how appealing it is, it is not good when the property leads the transaction, rather than the buyer's best interests leading the choice of property. An investor should not buy anything just to have something, or because interest rates are low. They should deal with someone who represents the buyer, not the seller.

People struggle with knowing who they can trust, and 'professionals' have broken that trust in the past. However, there are professional experts out there who will do the right thing, disclose their fees, and be independent/objective.

What to Look For

What investors should look for in a property depends on their individual circumstances and goals. Obviously, there are some common things you should look at, such as a trend in certain data, supply and demand, population, proximity to 'good' infrastructure, and a suitable dwelling for the demographic in that area that rents out easily.

Sometimes developers will calculate the living space based on the measurement around the outer shell. However, this is best judged by looking at the internal dimensions and not including the thickness of the walls. This can create a big discrepancy between the actual living space and what the developer claims as living space. If you do buy a really small dwelling, under 50 sq. m, you are going to have fewer people who want to buy it in the future. It is riskier, which means it may be hard to obtain finance.

There are many ramifications for buying the wrong type of property. From a lending point of view, if it is hard for you to get a loan on a certain property, when you eventually sell it, it may be hard or harder for the next person to buy it as well (possibly due to finance limitations). You may end up with a limited resale market and, therefore, lose some profit because you have to lower the price.

In fact, you may also be limited in how much you can borrow based on the type of dwelling. If you can only borrow 60% of the property value, you have to put in much more of your own money. This will present future problems in building your portfolio, because you have lost the opportunity to use that money elsewhere. It is a huge opportunity cost to use an unnecessary amount of equity in a property.

Some people do not want to affect their lifestyle with too many out-of-pocket expense. This risk is more prevalent if you buy the wrong established property. The risks are higher repairs, higher maintenance costs, and less depreciation, among others. But, you can still buy established dwellings and reduce the impact on your lifestyle if you have a buyer's agent to help you. By doing so, you decrease your risk of buying something that needs extensive repairs or maintenance.

Points to Consider when Buying

1. *Seek advice from a suitably qualified and insured individual who represents the buyer.*
2. *Thoroughly research everything.*
3. *Have a plan.*
4. *Start with your goals and work backwards.*
5. *Implement a finance strategy with the help of a property advisor.*
6. *Avoid property marketing companies.*
7. *Research key criteria, which include the number of days on market, potential for capital growth, vacancy rates, population growth, supply and demand, percentage of investors in the area, infrastructure, and suitable dwelling for the demographic.*
8. *Have a suitable strategy for meeting your individual needs; whether new or existing property suits your plan better, as well as capital growth versus cash flow, and inner city or regional. They all have their merits, but not all are suitable for everyone.*

What You Should Know About Spruikers

At least real estate agents are honest about their goals and what they are trying to do (most of the time). They are clear that they are selling a specific property. The derogatory term 'spruiker' refers to property marketing companies (generally).

They typically do not disclose what they earn.

There are many things wrong with spruikers;

- *Investors are drawn in by the tales they tell.*
- *A property will be sold to you off a stock list.*
- *They will tell you how wonderful off-the-plan apartments are.*
- *How wonderful living in a city is.*
- *How wonderful the house and land estates are.*

They only tell you part of the story. Such properties may grow in value, but you need someone to filter out the crap and separate the good ones to help achieve the results you are looking for. They must have no vested interest in one location, one strategy, one or a few developers, or one or a few stock lists.

It is vitally important that you make yourself aware of what is going on behind the scenes and the motives behind what property marketing companies are doing. Many of these property marketing companies are incentivised to promote a certain building. Their advice can be based on a large bonus they could receive in return.

Throwaway lines like, "Property has doubled every seven to ten years" will be used. In many areas it has, but it may not continue that way in the next ten or twenty years. The areas that have that sort of growth may become harder to find. Often, new areas have a huge amount of supply, so the sheer cost of holding a property for the short- or medium-term becomes untenable if the investor has to drop their rent to compete.

If you have been invited to a seminar where you are basically locked in a room with somebody who is trying to put you into a property, and it feels as though things are happening too quickly, they are building things up, and they are pushing you to make a decision, it is a dead giveaway that you are dealing with a property marketing company. Just walk away from them. Do your research and double-check.

Many people do not have the time or the knowledge of how and where to go for the research, or how to interpret it. They do not know what data is important, what data is not important, and what data should be looked at in conjunction with other data.

Therefore, do not just do your own research. Get someone representing you, the buyer, to do the research, help you, and educate you in that process. Otherwise, you risk giving up because you run out of time, or take the easy option and listen to the wrong person, convincing yourself that it will all be okay.

One of the best ways to tell whether you are dealing with a spruiker or someone you can trust is to look at their documentation to determine if they disclose what they are earning to you. If they do, make sure they have insurance to give advice, rather than only having insurance for selling a property.

People have a right to earn money, but property spruikers do not typically disclose what they are earning and that is wrong. It is unethical and counterintuitive to how a compliant model should be (a compliant model was described earlier; represent the buyer, disclose any commissions, be insured, follow a code of conduct, be adequately qualified and experienced).

Anyone can get insurance to sell property. I use that as a point of difference because every mortgage broker or financial planner would typically have professional indemnity insurance, as would accountants, lawyers, doctors, and cleaners.

In property, insurance is harder to get, so the ones that do have insurance for property investment advice are the ones classified by the insurers as a more acceptable risk, and therefore, safer for a buyer to use (in my opinion).

Anyone who offers to find you only new property, should be a suspected spruiker, not a buyers agent, not a property advisor, and most not fully and wholeistically buyer centric.

To be fully or wholeistically buyer centric, established properties, different strategies, different property types should all be considered and included in the service providers offering. The professional you work with should thoroughly understand your needs and goals before setting out to source a property for you.

Some people are very good at pretending they do this, only to circle round and come back to their limited supply of stock, usually in one area, one part of town, or one state.

A true property advisor would have access to new and established properties across Australia, and certainly across the Eastern seaboard where 80% of the population is located. Please understand that some of the properties spruikers are selling are excellent, but you need an objective viewpoint to assess and review the property.

Avoid the vertically-integrated system. This involves several people, such as a conveyancer, a broker, a salesman, and maybe an accountant. They usually only have access to a certain few lenders who they know may provide a loan for the specific product they have to sell. That does not mean it is a good product. The fact that there are a limited number of lenders that will lend on that product is a giveaway that you should not buy it.

A vertically-integrated company promotes the fact that they are a one stop shop and they do everything for you. However, they often have undisclosed fees, or disclosed fees that are very high, which they profit from. They have vested interests in what they are doing, rather than keeping the buyer's interests essential to the situation.

Vertically-integrated models are self-centric, rather than buyer-centric. You should deal with independent conveyancers, mortgage brokers, and accountants. In a vertically-integrated company, everyone is singing the same tune and you are none the wiser.

Take your plans to your accountant, who can hopefully provide you some better advice. An independent broker would be able to assess whether you should avoid that property from a lending point of view.

The conveyancer in a vertically-integrated model will normally charge much more money under the guise that you need someone to understand the contract. If the contract is that hard to understand, do not sign it. Eventually, when you want to sell the property, you run the risk that fewer people will want to buy it from you.

Why Not to Approach Financial Advisors for Property Advice

Many people, when they think of obtaining advice, turn to financial planners or financial advisors. Let's bust the myth that they can help you with giving you advice on a specific property. They may be able to allocate a portion of your funds toward property in general as an asset class, but they cannot provide advice on any specific property under their financial services license.

The financial planning industry deals with investment products (securities). Currently, the Australian Securities and Investments Commission (ASIC) does not recognise property as an investment security.

ASIC (an independent Commonwealth Government body) contributes to the wellbeing and reputation of the Australian economy, helping investors become more informed and confident by ensuring fairness and transparency in Australia's financial markets. Their responsibility includes enforcing and giving effect to the law, making information available to the public on companies and other bodies.

Shares, managed funds, superannuation structures, and insurance are the main financial products (investment securities) that ASIC regulates under a financial services license, and what financial planners may be able to advise on. It doesn't include specific property, nor does it include credit advice, like mortgages.

A good financial planner, in my opinion, will generally provide advice on the allocation of funds to property, as an asset class. Unfortunately there has been considerable corruption in the financial planning space with some institutional financial planners providing inappropriate advice to investor, just to line their pockets.

Many financial advisors work for institutions, and these institutions often govern what their advisors offer you, by way of the product they recommend. They can conveniently recommend their own institutionally-owned products. This may severely limit you from what is available in the marketplace.

Some financial planners give the industry a bad name. They receive kickbacks from developers by passing their client over to buy one of their properties. These are often, if not always, undisclosed. We are talking about commissions of 2% or more, plus additional incentives (such as an extra 1%, or bonuses) for certain projects.

Unlike regulated industries, such as accounting and financial planning, working for a property marketing company (as distinct from operating as a traditional real estate agent) does not require a great deal of education, experience, or studies completed.

Marketing investment property, put simply, requires nothing but the ability to sell, and this is meant to be a wake-up call and warning! Literally anyone can be involved in property, which has resulted in many predators in the field.

The property market has also attracted highly ethical people, who are very professional. With so much noise and distraction everywhere, it is (all too often) difficult to spot the difference between the good and the bad.

Why Engage the Services of a True Advisor?

To provide the best opportunity for investors to benefit from engaging our services, we tailor advice within the scope of a risk profile, which matches the client with a property by comprehensively evaluating investment structures, property investment strategy, market conditions, and climate.

Considerable due diligence for the client, combined with property choices that have been researched and sourced, is provided in the form of a Tailored Property Investment Advice Document. We facilitate the ability for investors, who have engaged our services, to make informed decisions based on the quality of a foundation of information.

We take into account the investor's goals, their lifestyle, and their finances to find suitable property choices for their circumstances. We state all major assumptions, similar to a financial plan or prospectus. All of our recommendations ignore emotion. Choices of property utilise information about the product's potential performance, allowing for several property choices to be considered, as they may all meet the client's risk profile.

The main point to recognise is that this all culminates in reducing the urgency to purchase a particular property, and it is therefore a more professional process. There are no glossy brochures with pretty pictures of all the wonderful inclusions, like stone benchtops, plush carpets, and shiny tiles.

Most investors just want to know the property will have good potential to grow in value, attract a good tenant, and be affordable.

The Australian Property Advisory Group Advice Method

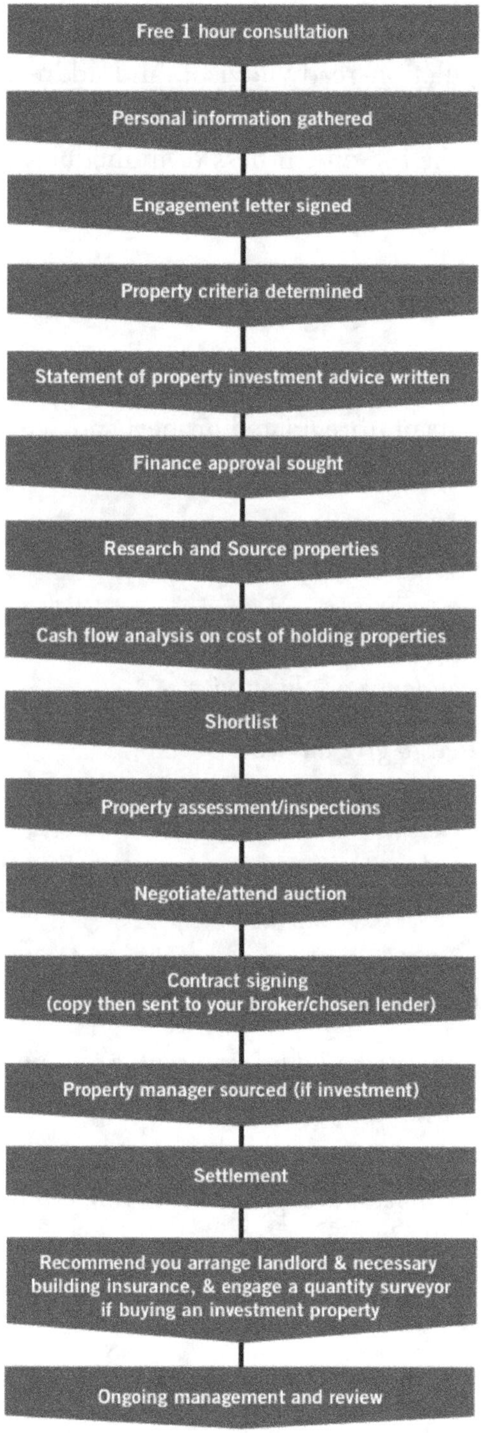

We help you by making sure you avoid situations where you might be given inflated performance projections, and experience pressure sales techniques that are designed to manipulate investors. All of this makes for a regulation-ready advisor, and addresses the concerns expressed by the Government, such as barriers of entry, consumer protection, and the big one: fitness of individuals practising in the industry.

In Summary

The Problems You Can Avoid

These are the traits of unregulated property advice personnel acting in a non-compliant manner:

- *vested interests between mortgage brokers, banks, and associates*
- *undisclosed commissions*
- *no independence or objectivity*
- *not insured to give advice*
- *represent the seller – not you, the buyer*
- *have a property already lined up to sell, with (possibly) some clever sales techniques to entice you to "sign up now."*

The Solution Available

- *you, the buyer, should be represented by someone with no direct relationship to the vendor and no property lined up to sell*
- *property choices are guided by you, your goals, risk appetite, and finance*
- *fees are disclosed, and your advisor(s) work to a strict code of ethics*

- *thorough research; analysis, not hearsay*
- *advisors with professional indemnity (PI) insurance*

The Value of This Solution

Modelling Tools are provided to help you

- *reduce risk*
- *keep and improve your lifestyle*
- *have access to property you may not have had before*
- *gain explanations and education regarding risks*
- *leverage off the advisor's education and experience*
- *realise that having a real property advisor is great insurance*
- *integrate strategies towards the goal of achieving a passive income in, or before, retirement.*

Final Word

You have come to the end of my book, and I am sure you have been able to take a great deal of benefit from having read it. The most important thing you could take away is to have a plan, and engage the services of a suitably qualified professional. Without these services, I believe many of you will struggle. It may be difficult to grow a portfolio of adequate size to suit your future needs. We have to live life for today, but also live life with tomorrow in mind.

This book should be read in conjunction with my other newly released book, the fifth instalment in the *Made Simple* series, entitled *Commercial Property and Residential Development Made Simple.*

Property investing is a journey – it should be an enjoyable, stress-free journey. If you want to reduce risk, improve potential, eliminate the stress and time in researching, sourcing, and negotiating for a property, and make money on the property, contact me via the details on the following page.

You may surprise yourself with what you can achieve if you dream big and take action.

Contact

If you would like assistance with buyer advocacy, property advice, or being put in contact with a suitably qualified professional for conveyancing, development, commercial finance, mortgage broking, insurance, financial planning, accounting, or property inspections, then contact me and I will endeavour to assist you.

Additionally, you may wish to purchase one of my first two books for the discounted rate of $14.99 (RRP $24.99):

Property Investing Made Simple

Property Finance Made Simple

If you quote 'discount19' you will receive 5% off of our buyer advocacy or property advisory services.

RESOURCES:

To obtain the 'Investment Readiness Questionnaire,' my *Blueprint to Property Investment Success* ©, and your own research checklist, please visit my website:

www.australianpropertyadvisorygroup.com.au

WEBSITES:

www.propertyinvestingmadesimple.com.au

www.propertyfinancemadesimple.net.au

www.australianpropertyadvisorygroup.com.au

www.the100kpropertyplan.com.au

EMAIL:

advice@australianpropertyadvisorygroup.com.au or Andrew@apag.com.au

PHONE:

1300 760901

SOCIAL MEDIA:

www.facebook.com/australianpropertyadvisorygroup

www.facebook.com/propertyfinancemadesimple/

www.facebook.com/Propertyinvestingmadesimple/

www.twitter.com/CrossleyAndrew

https://www.linkedin.com/in/andrewccrossley/

Notes

www.ingramcontent.com/pod-product-compliance
Lightning Source LLC
LaVergne TN
LVHW022215200926
848481LV00006B/1981
9781925830668